Dept

The Rise and Fall of the British Empire

Teacher's Support Guide

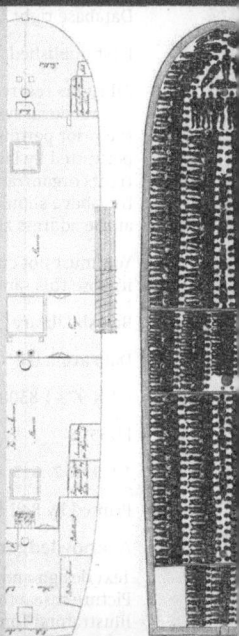

Emma Wilkes

OXFORD
UNIVERSITY PRESS

OXFORD
UNIVERSITY PRESS

Great Clarendon Street, Oxford OX2 6DP

Oxford University Press is a department of the University of Oxford.
It furthers the University's objective of excellence in research, scholarship,
and education by publishing worldwide in Oxford   New York Auckland
Cape Town   Dar es Salaam   Hong Kong   Karachi   Kuala Lumpur   Madrid
Melbourne   Mexico City   Nairobi   New Delhi   Shanghai   Taipei   Toronto

With offices in
Argentina Austria Brazil Chile Czech Republic France Greece
Guatemala Hungary Italy Japan Poland Portugal Singapore
South Korea Switzerland Thailand Turkey Ukraine Vietnam

Oxford is a registered trade mark of Oxford University Press
in the UK and in certain other countries

© Emma Wilkes 2010

The moral rights of the authors have been asserted

Database right Oxford University Press (maker)

First published 2010

All rights reserved. No part of this publication may be reproduced, stored
in a retrieval system, or transmitted, in any form or by any means, without
the prior permission in writing of Oxford University Press, or as expressly
permitted by law, or under terms agreed with the appropriate reprographics
rights organization. Enquiries concerning reproduction outside the scope of
the above should be sent to the Rights Department, Oxford University Press,
at the address above

You must not circulate this book in any other binding or cover and you must
impose this same condition on any acquirer

British Library Cataloguing in Publication Data

Data available

ISBN 978-1-85008-551-5

FD5515

10 9 8 7 6 5 4

Printed by Bell & Bain Ltd, Glasgow.

Acknowledgements

Text design and layout: Anthony Finch
Picture researcher: Cathy Hurren
Illustrators: Tony Randell and Clive Wakfer
Cover design: Anthony Finch and Rosa Capacchione
Cover images: © iStockphoto.com/nicoolay (left); © INTERFOTO/Alamy (centre); © North Wind Picture Archives/Alamy (right); p.8 Topfoto/ Granger Collection, New York; p.10 Bridgeman Art Library/Trustees of the Bedford Estate, Woburn Abbey (top), www.heritage-history.com (bottom); p.19 Interfoto/ AAA Collection; p.25 © Mary Evans Picture Library/Alamy; p.28 William Wilberforce watching a master mistreat his slaves at the dockside in Liverpool by Doughty, C.L. (1913-85) Private Collection/ © Look and Learn/ The Bridgeman Art Library Nationality / copyright status: British / copyright unknown (top), © The Art Gallery Collection/Alamy (middle), Landing cargo of African slaves, Jamestown, Virginia, 1619 (litho) by American School, (17th century) Private Collection/ Peter Newark American Pictures/ The Bridgeman Art Library Nationality / copyright status: American / out of copyright (bottom); p.30 The Art Gallery Collection/Alamy; p.32 Lebrecht Music and Arts Photo Library/Alamy; p.35 Pictorial Press Ltd/Alamy; p.38 © iStockphoto.com/Courtney Navey; p.40 Copyright 2010 photolibrary.com (top), Copyright 2010 photolibrary.com (middle), © iStockphoto.com/Holger Mette (bottom); p.45 The 7th Bengal Infantry on Parade, the Anglo-Indian Army of the 1880s (colour litho), Simkin, Richard (1840-1926) (after) / Private Collection / Peter Newark Pictures / The Bridgeman Art Library; p.48 © 19th era/Alamy; p.49 Mary Evans Picture Library; p.53 Mary Evans Picture Library; p.61 © iStockphoto.com/RMAX (top), Illustrated London News Ltd/Mary Evans (middle), London Stereoscopic Company/Getty Images (bottom); p.65 © Roger Fletcher/Alamy; p.72 The Signing of the Treaty of Waitangi by Captain Hobson and the Maori chiefs in 1840, 1938 (oil on canvas) by King, Marcus (20th century) Alexander Turnbull Library, Wellington, New Zealand/ The Bridgeman Art Library; p.73 Imagestate/ HIP/British Library; p.74 Mirrorpix (left), Ministry of Defence (right); p.75 Swim Ink 2, LLC/CORBIS (top), HIP/ Imagestate (bottom); p.83 The Defence of Rorke's Drift, 1880 (oil on canvas) by Neuville, Alphonse Marie de (1835-85) Art Gallery of New South Wales, Sydney, Australia/ The Bridgeman Art Library; p.85 Mary Evans Picture Library

The websites recommended in this publication were correct at the time of going to press; however, websites may have been removed or web addresses changed since that time. OUP has made every attempt to suggest websites that are reliable and appropriate for students' use. It is not unknown for unscrupulous individuals to put unsuitable material on websites that may be accessed by students. Teachers should check all websites before allowing students to access them. OUP is not responsible for the content of external websites.

Every effort has been made to contact copyright holders of material used in this publication. If any copyright holder has been overlooked, we will be pleased to make any necessary arrangements.

Contents

Introduction 5

What is an empire?
The rise and fall of empires 6
The largest empire in the world 7

The Big Question: How did the British Empire begin?
An age of discovery 8
Beginnings 9

The Big Question: How did the Empire grow?
The growth of the British Empire 10
Which explorer? 11
The story of the British Empire 12
In your own words… 13
Empire bingo! 15
The Empire so far 16
Empire crossword 17

Depth Study: British America
Join us… 18
Are you tough enough? 19
The first English settlers 20
Life in the colonies: who came first? 21
Why on earth are we all here? 22
North America today 23
What did your new land grow? 24
The *Mayflower* 25
The triangular trade (1) 26
The triangular trade (2) 27
Every brick in the city of Liverpool 28
The Boston Tea Party 29
Boston times 30
There was an old lady lived over the sea 31
Independence! 32
America wordsearch 33
The American Story 34

The Big Question: Should Britain make up for its role in slavery?
Olaudah Equiano 35
Slavery sucks 36
Slavery divides Europe 37
The compensation debate 38
A British response: what would you say? 39

Depth Study: India
Once upon a time… 40
A divided nation 41
Conquest 42
How to make a fortune from trade 43
Who owned what? 44
The Battle of Plassey 45

Life as a Sepoy	46
Remember Cawnpore	47
The Queen speaks	48
Who was Curzon?	49
I write on behalf of…	50
What impact?	51
The growth of Britain's control over India	52
The salt tax	53
Obituary	54
Whose burden?	55
Timeline of India's history	56
India puzzle	57
India word square	58
India wordsearch	59
The Indian story	60

The Big Question: So how big was the British Empire?

When did the British take control?	61
The sun never sets	62

The Big Question: What did the Empire do for Britain?

How did the Empire benefit?	63
Other benefits	64

Depth Study: A land down under

The life and travels of Cook	65
Your Royal Highness	66
A little bit of England	67
Transportation nation	68
Adventure or invasion?	69
Pemulwuy	70
The Stolen Generations	71
The birth of a nation	72
Australia word square	73
What about New Zealand?	74
The Australian story	75

The Big Question: Did the Empire strike back?

The Empire strikes back	76

The Big Question: Did the Empire help win two World Wars?

Who were they?	77
The Empire needs you!	78

Depth Study: Africa

Africa wordsearch	79
Britain's African Empire	80
Zulu (1)	81
Zulu (2)	82
An historical snapshot	83

The Big Question: What is the legacy of the British Empire?

Unfit for duty	84
Legacy of the Empire	85

The Big Question: Was the British Empire a good or a bad thing?

Positive or negative?	86
British overseas territories	87
Get out of your seats!	88

Introduction

This History series has become a popular and well-loved approach to KS3 History, blending the acquisition and development of skills with entertaining, fun-filled themes and narrative. The Depth Study titles give a more detailed insight into a section of British and world history, which allows teachers to delve deeper into topics and themes of particular interest.

Using this teacher's support guide

This teacher's support guide features a variety of activities to support and extend the information and activities in the Student's Book. Where there are specific links, these are mentioned on the worksheet itself.

Some worksheets provide support for specific activities; for example, a structure to help students plan and draft their responses to challenging tasks, or additional information to add a further level of complexity to students' answers. Other worksheets provide new material, either in the form of complimentary information in relation to the depth study, or through providing new activities to consolidate the learning in the Student's Book.

Active and independent learners

Many of the worksheets in this book are designed to promote active and collaborative learning approaches. They can promote paired and small group work as well as encourage students to carry out their own research online or at their local public or school library. Most worksheets are freestanding and can be used for homework or for extending issues/areas covered in the Student's Book.

A flexible approach

The worksheets encourage a variety of methods of learning; in fact, as students work through them they will notice a wide variety of different types of activities. They have not been written to a single formula or aimed at any specific ability range: you could use one worksheet as a starter activity with one particular teaching group whilst the same activity might be used as an extension or homework task with another. Indeed the worksheets have not been written as a collection of starters, plenary or extension tasks. Instead the tasks have been produced to allow teachers to use any task in any particular way.

All worksheets are provided on the accompanying CD-ROM as PDFs and editable Word documents. There are also additional digital resources to add variety of presentation to the tasks.

The rise and fall of empires

☞ Do some research and decide which date each of the empires listed below existed. Then cut out the boxes and the timeline, stick the timeline on an A4 piece of paper and stick the empires next to the correct date.

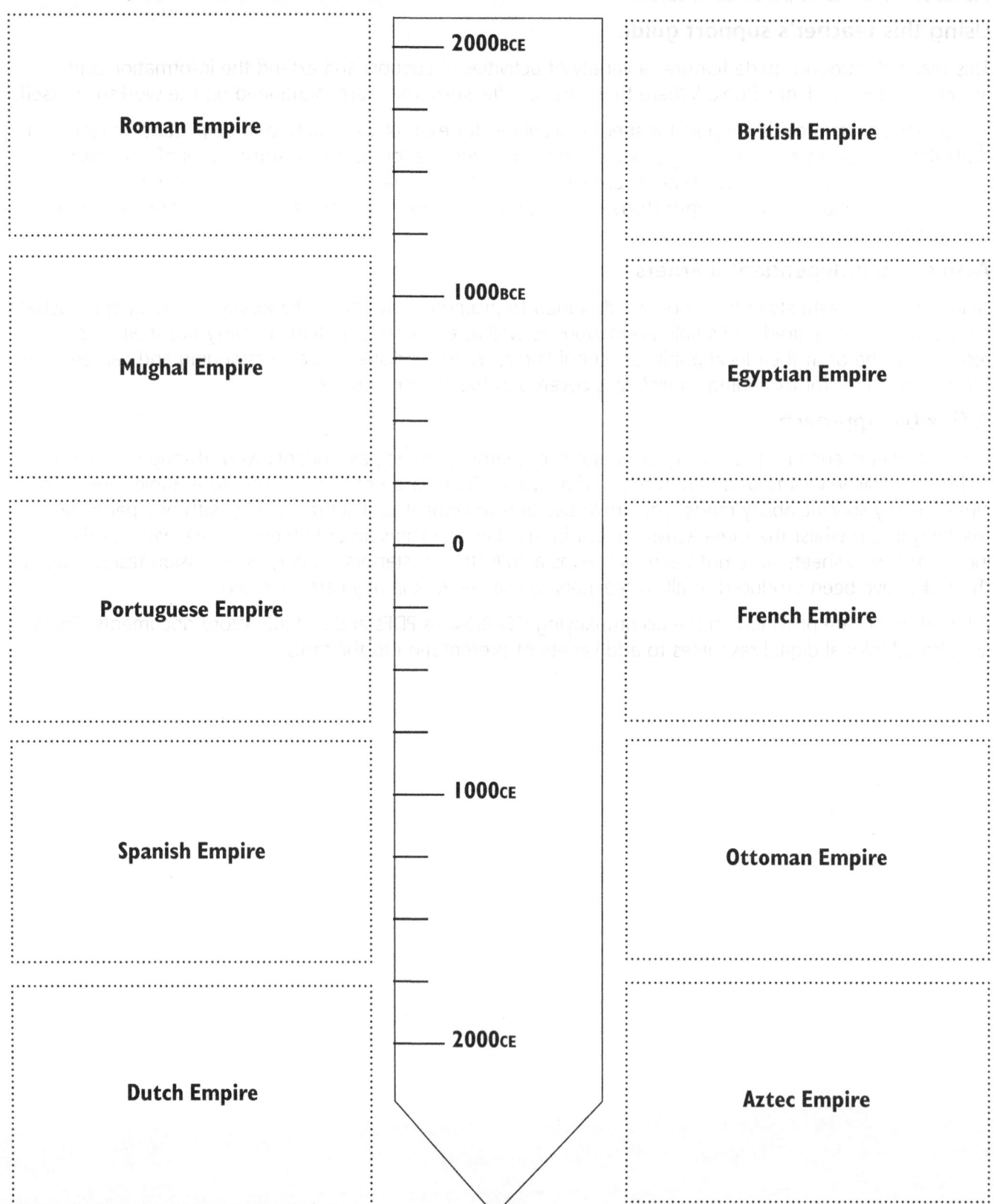

Extension Activity: From your research suggest which empires were the most successful. For example you could base your opinion on their size or the length of time they survived.

The largest empire in the world

From small beginnings in the early 1600s the British Empire went from strength to strength to become the largest empire in the world. By 1900 Britain ruled over 450 million people living in 56 different countries.

☞ Use the three maps below to chart the growth of the British Empire from 1750 to 1900 by shading in the countries the British Empire controlled at that time.

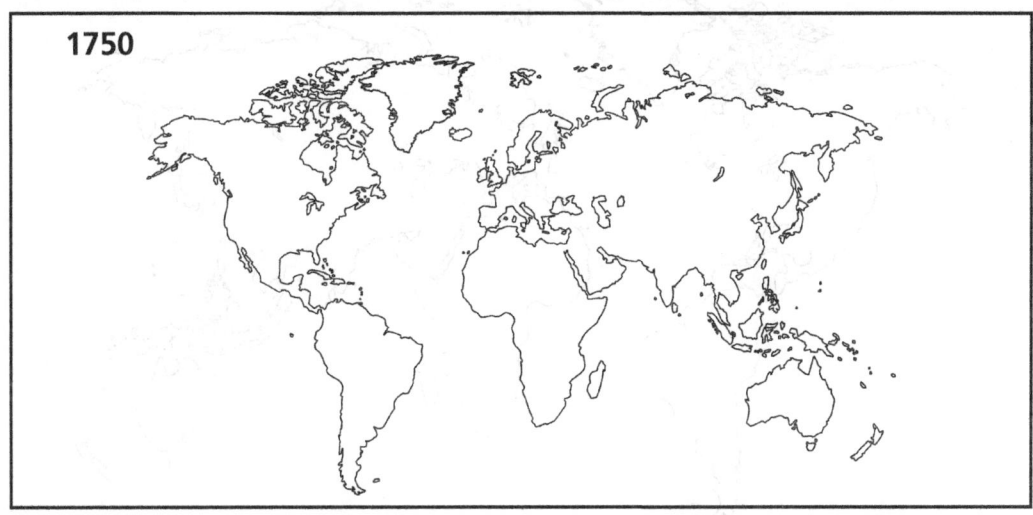

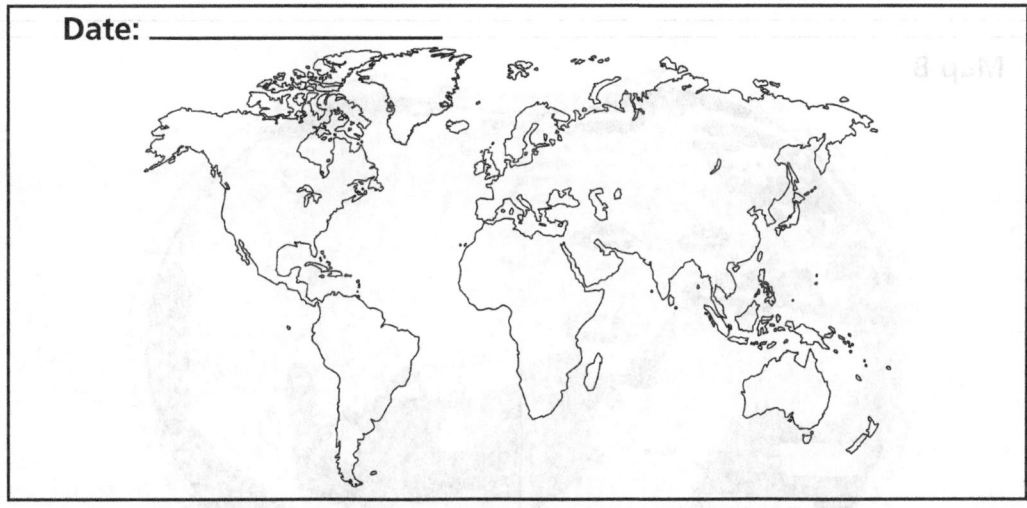

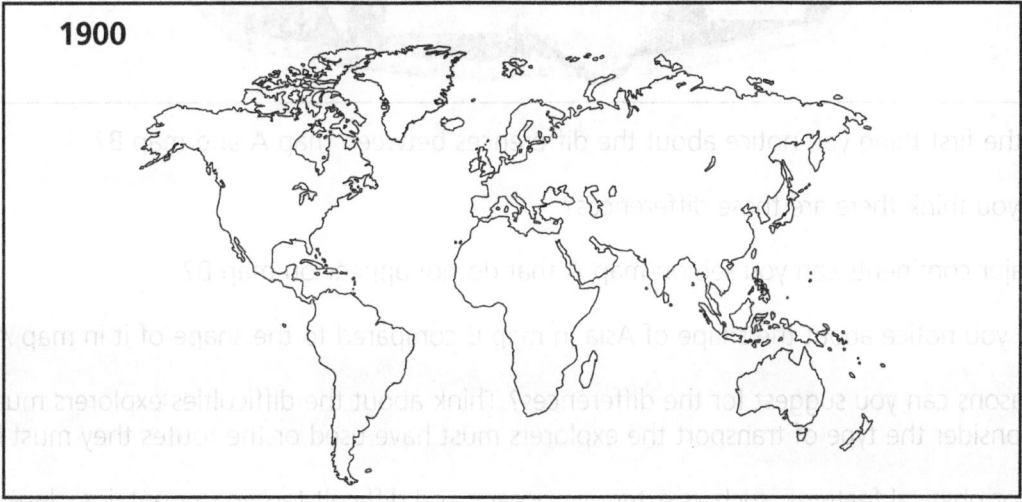

Extension Activity: Study the maps you have completed. What do you notice about them? Are there any specific areas where Britain ruled more countries? How does this compare to other empires you have learnt about, such as the Spanish Empire?

© Oxford University Press (copiable page)

An age of discovery

☞ As the kings of great empires were keen to find new lands, the ideas of how our world was shaped began to change. Study the maps below and then answer the questions in your workbook.

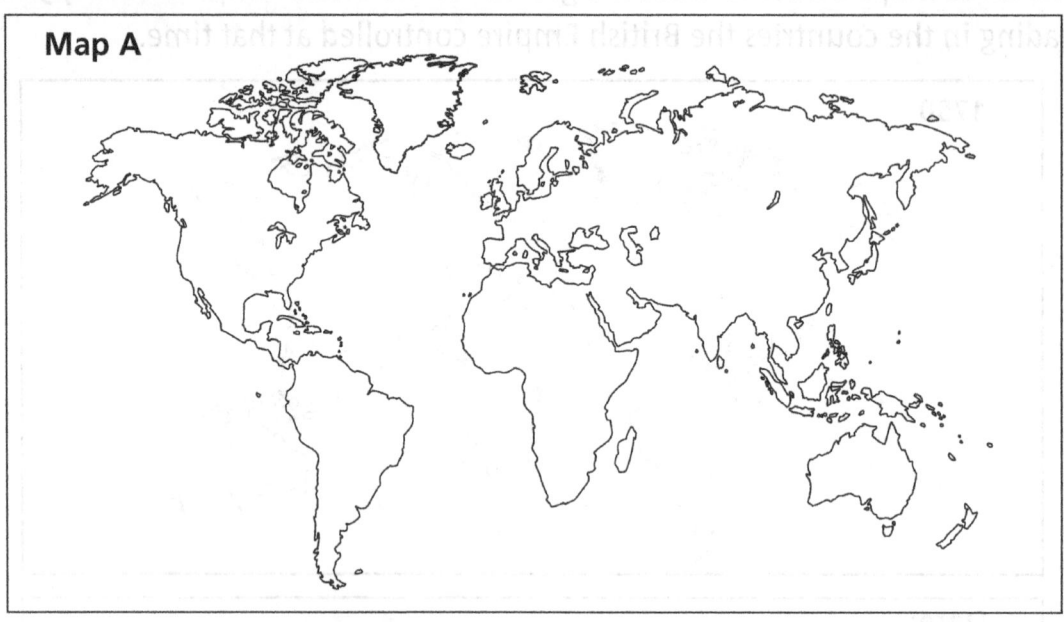

Map A

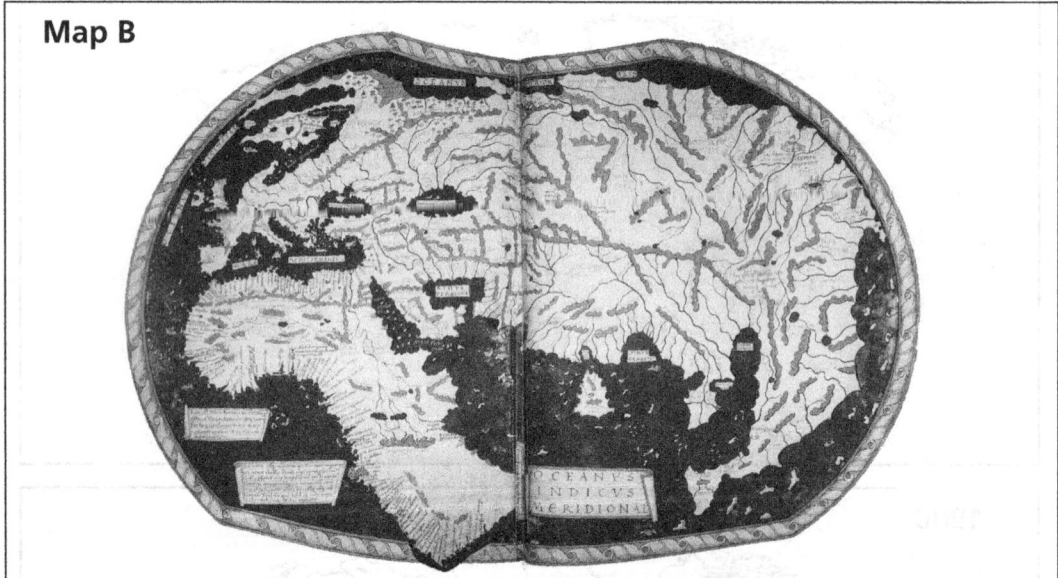

Map B

1. What is the first thing you notice about the differences between map A and map B?

2. Why do you think there are these differences?

3. What major continents can you see on map A that do not appear on map B?

4. What do you notice about the shape of Asia in map B compared to the shape of it in map A?

5. What reasons can you suggest for the differences? Think about the difficulties explorers must have faced. Consider the type of transport the explorers must have used or the routes they must have taken.

6. 'The major physical features, such as extensive oceans and difficult terrain (mountains, deserts, ice and dangerous river crossings) would have impacted on the travellers of the time.' Suggest how this statement and the modes of transport used at the time may have helped to influence Martellus' map (map B).

Beginnings

☞ John Cabot has been set the task of funding new lands for England, but he needs men to sail with him. Complete the advertisement below to find men to join him on his voyage.

Think carefully about the following when designing your advert:
- How can you encourage men to join him? What would they find in new lands?
- What other lands have been found by other explorers and how successful might John Cabot and his men be?
- What type of men would Cabot need? What skills might be appropriate?
- What fears would the men have about joining the journey (remember, many Europeans thought the world was flat)?

The growth of the British Empire

The following sources are related to the growth of the British Empire during Tudor times – but what do they tell you?

☞ **Annotate the following sources, paying particular attention to what they tell you about the growth of the British Empire. Give reasons for highlighting particular features in each.**

Remember to think carefully about the purpose of these pictures: what are they trying to tell you? Are they a true reflection of events that took place? Are they biased in any way?

Source A: The Armada portrait of Elizabeth I, painted by George Gower in 1588.

Source B: Painting of Sir Humphrey Gilbert.

The Big Question: How did the British Empire grow?

Which explorer?

Below are three key explorers who were part of Queen Elizabeth I's plans to gain land in faraway places. But what do we know about them?

☞ **Surrounding each explorer are some interesting facts – but which explorer do they belong to? Draw a line from each fact to the explorer it relates to. You will need to conduct your own research to complete this activity.**

Extension Activity: See if you can add two more facts about each of these explorers. Try to make them as interesting and as relevant as possible!

The story of the British Empire

☞ Read the following statements about the growth of the British Empire during the reign of Elizabeth I. Cut them out and stick them on a piece of A4 paper in the correct order to tell the story of the British Empire.

The settlers were attacked by hostile tribesmen and those who escaped fled by sea, never to be seen again.

A second group of travellers (117 of them) arrived in 1587 and the first English child was born in America soon after.

England needed to find new ways to reach China travelling north of Russia, but famous explorers were unable to find new routes.

In 1577 Sir Francis Drake made a successful attempt to travel around the world.

Other countries could boast the discovery of tobacco, tomatoes and rum; England, however, could only boast finding cod!

When John White returned the colony had been deserted. The only clue as to their fate was a post carved with the word 'Croatoan'.

Sir Humphrey Gilbert was given permission to set up a colony in Newfoundland (Canada) – he claimed hundreds of miles of land.

Queen Elizabeth I sent another explorer, Sir Walter Raleigh, to start another colony, which would be known as Virginia.

Life became difficult again and John White returned home to gather fresh supplies and fetch help.

Unfortunately people didn't settle in Newfoundland and returned home.

Nearly 100 settlers started new lives here, but a lack of supplies and inexperience made things difficult.

In the mid-1950s Spain had control over much of the Americas; this included countries like Jamaica, Peru and Cuba.

As he travelled, Sir Francis Drake landed on the western coast of America, claiming it for England – along with 26 tons of silver, which he stole from the Spanish en route.

Queen Elizabeth I encouraged new adventurers, like Sir Francis Drake, to steal gold and silver from the Spanish ships. Along with their stolen goods came valuable maps and sea charts.

The Big Question: How did the British Empire grow?

In your own words...

☞ Over the next two pages is a series of cartoons that tell the story of the growth of the British Empire during the reign of Elizabeth I. Cut them out and stick them on an A3 piece of paper in the correct order. Write a caption for each to help tell the story using words from the Word Bank to help you.

Word Bank

- Spain • Trade • China • Sir Francis Drake • New World • Privateers
- Newfoundland • Virginia • Colony • John White • Roanoke

© Oxford University Press (copiable page)

The Big Question: How did the British Empire grow?

In your own words...

Empire bingo!

☞ This game is designed to test your knowledge of key words from your studies on the British Empire. Below are a number of words related to this topic. Choose nine of these words and write them in the bingo card below. As your teacher reads out a definition, decide if you have the word written on your bingo card – if you have, put a tick against it. When you have ticked all of your words (a full house) shout out "Bingo!" – will you be the first to win?

Word Bank

- Colony • Dependency • Explorer • Empire • Columbus • New World
- Americas • Renaissance • Virginia • Dominion • John Cabot • Newfoundland
- Sir Humphrey Gilbert • Settlers • Privateers • Natives • Redskins • Sir Walter Raleigh

The Big Question: How did the British Empire grow?

The Empire so far

☞ The following words about the British Empire can be found in the wordsearch below. Look carefully to see if you can find them all. When you have completed the wordsearch write a definition for each of the words.

Word Bank

- Americas • Britain • Cabot • Civilizations • Colonies • Colony • Columbus
- Dependency • Discovery • Dominion • Drake • Elizabeth • Empire • European
- Gilbert • Hawkins • Independence • Portugal • Privateers • Spain

Y	S	B	U	B	Z	O	Q	N	H	J	R	H	W	S
R	A	M	E	R	I	C	A	S	T	O	B	A	C	P
E	C	H	G	I	B	O	A	R	E	Q	F	W	I	A
V	G	B	L	T	W	L	M	E	B	T	D	K	V	I
O	I	X	G	A	T	O	S	E	A	P	O	I	I	N
C	L	O	M	I	L	N	K	T	Z	I	M	N	L	D
S	B	A	Z	N	A	I	E	A	I	E	I	S	I	E
I	E	H	R	F	Q	E	O	V	L	L	N	Z	Z	P
D	R	A	K	E	Y	S	Y	I	E	I	I	H	A	E
C	T	N	V	N	E	L	D	R	I	Z	O	J	T	N
E	N	T	O	M	C	K	P	P	F	V	N	G	I	D
W	D	L	P	O	R	T	U	G	A	L	I	P	O	E
U	O	I	M	N	A	E	P	O	R	U	E	K	N	N
C	R	E	D	S	X	C	O	L	U	M	B	U	S	C
E	C	N	E	D	N	E	P	E	D	N	I	J	R	Y

The Big Question: How did the British Empire grow?

Empire crossword

☞ Use the clues to complete this crossword puzzle.

Across

3 Controlled lots of land in North America before defeat in the Seven Years War (6)
5 Taken from here to a life of slavery (6)
7 The month in which Independence Day occurs (4)
8 _____ of Independence, 1776 (11)
11 They had a tea party in 1773 (6)
13 Stars and _____: New American flag (7)
16 British city that grew rich from the profits of slavery (9)
17 British slave trader (7)
18 A profitable crop (7)
19 The first American president (10)

Down

1 Colony named after Queen Elizabeth I (8)
2 A 1607 settlement (9)
4 European who discovered the Americas (8)
6 _____ Americans: people living in America long before the Europeans arrived (6)
9 American parliament (8)
10 Leader of the British Army, beaten by the Americans in 1781 (10)
12 The number of colonies (8)
14 A tribal princess (10)
15 '_____ World': an early nickname for the Americas (3)

Join us...

You have been put in charge of promoting Jamestown. Your job is to encourage people to come and live in America, to help build the colony.

☞ Write a magazine advert to 'sell' the new life in America to those at home in England. Try to include as many benefits as possible, for example: lifestyle, jobs, wealth, food, land, and native people. Think about how you may tackle the negatives, such as disease, unrest, and hard working conditions.

Join Us...

Are you tough enough?

☞ Study the following sources, from page 15 of the Student's Book, which describe what life was like for the earlier settlers. What do they tell you about their first impressions of their new found home?

Source C: From Nova Britannia by R.I. 1609

"It is inhabited by wild and savage people that live all over the forests. They have no law but native and wear clothes made from the skin of beasts and some go naked. The better sorts have houses, but poor ones have neither Arts nor Science, but are generally loving and gentle and do entertain us with kindness. They are easy to be brought to good but would happily like better conditions."

Source D: *By the Virginia Company.*

"The land can easily sustain us – there are plenty of fish, deer, stags and rabbits, with many fruits and roots good for meat. There are valleys and plains streaming with sweet springs, there are hills and mountains full of hidden treasure not yet searched."

Source E: *A picture claiming to show what life was like for settlers in America.*

☞ Annotate Source E to explain what it tells you about the new lands discovered.

Extension Activity: Do you think these sources give a reliable view of life in the New World? Why do you think they may have presented this view to those at home in England?

The first English settlers

☞ Imagine you are an Englishman arriving for the first time in North America and write two diary entries to describe what it is like to become one of the first English settlers there. In the first entry think about what you saw as you arrived (use Source B from page 14 of the Student's Book to help you). As your life in America starts, write the second diary entry about the problems you and other settlers face. What reasons have you found to stay? Use words from the Word Bank to help you.

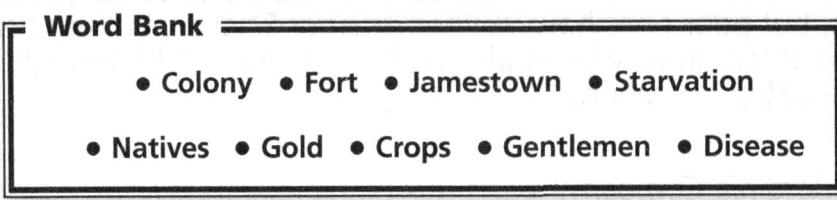

Word Bank

- Colony • Fort • Jamestown • Starvation
- Natives • Gold • Crops • Gentlemen • Disease

Life in the colonies: who came first?

The first settlers in America came from many different European countries; but when did they arrive and in what order did they slowly take control of the different territories?

☞ The map below shows the European invasion of America. Colour in the key, using different colours for each country, then use those colours to fill in the arrows on the map to show which European country invaded which area. Then complete the dates.

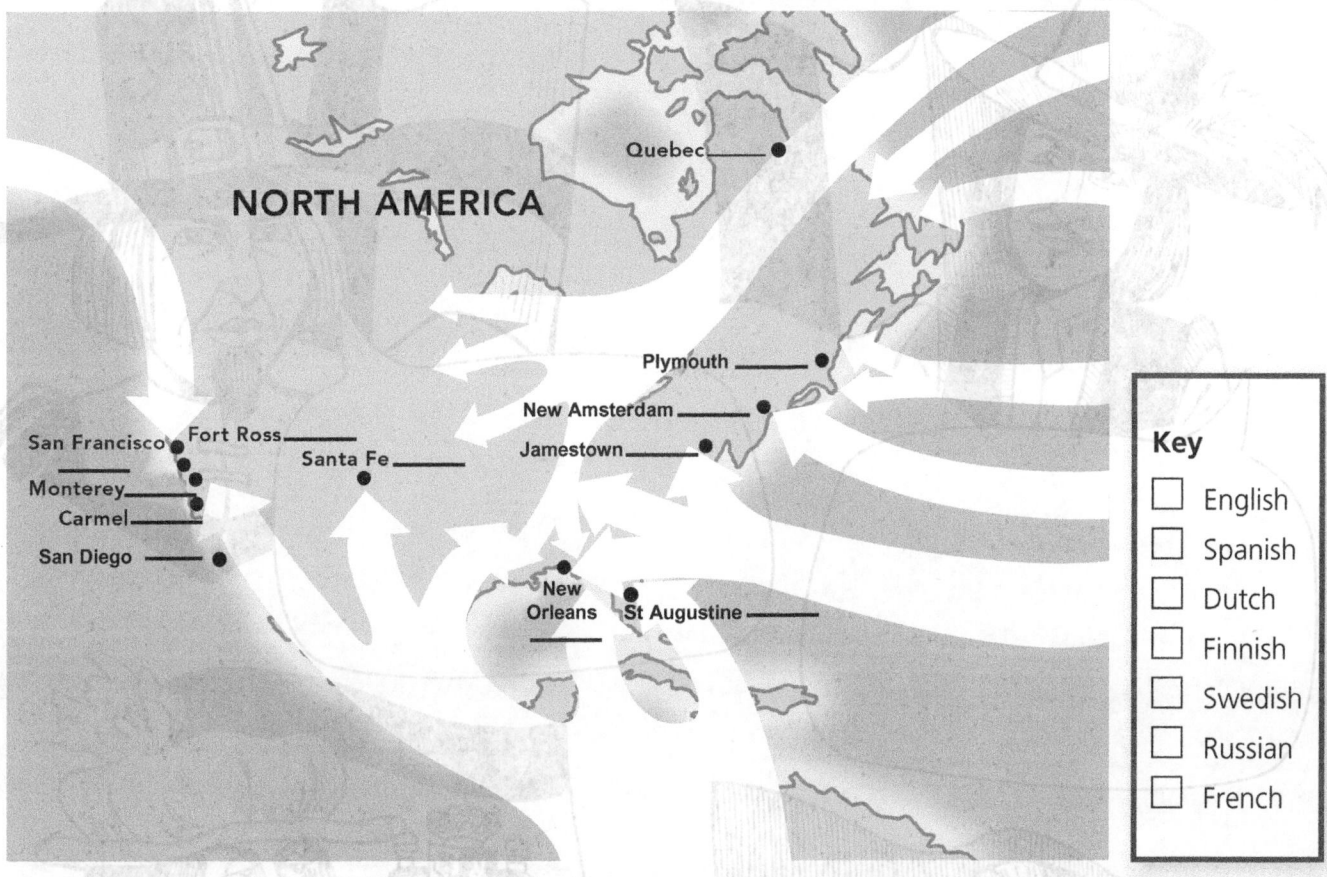

☞ Listed below are a number of territories in North America. See if you can put them in chronological order of when they were invaded by cutting them out and sticking them in your workbook. Colour code them according to who invaded which area: use the key to help you.

| San Francisco | Monterey | Carmel | San Diego | Fort Ross | Santa Fe |
| New Orleans | St Augustine | Jamestown | New Amsterdam | Plymouth | Quebec |

Extension Activity: What links can you find with the original settlers to these places nowadays? Use the Internet or the library to help you.

© Oxford University Press (copiable page)   **Depth Study: British America**

Why on earth are we all here?

The first settlers to arrive in America were from many different European countries, but they all had different reasons for wanting to make the journey.

☞ Below are a number of travellers from various places in Europe. Write a short speech for each to explain why they travelled across the sea to new lands

Extension Activity: Find out why people from Sweden and Finland also travelled to America.

22 Depth Study: British America © Oxford University Press (copiable page)

North America today

☞ Below is a map of the east coast of North America today. Using what you have learnt about early settlements and the regions along the east coast known as the thirteen colonies, what evidence can you find of these early settlers today? Do any areas still have the same names? Are there any place names similar to those in England today? Use an atlas and the Internet to help with your research so you can complete the map.

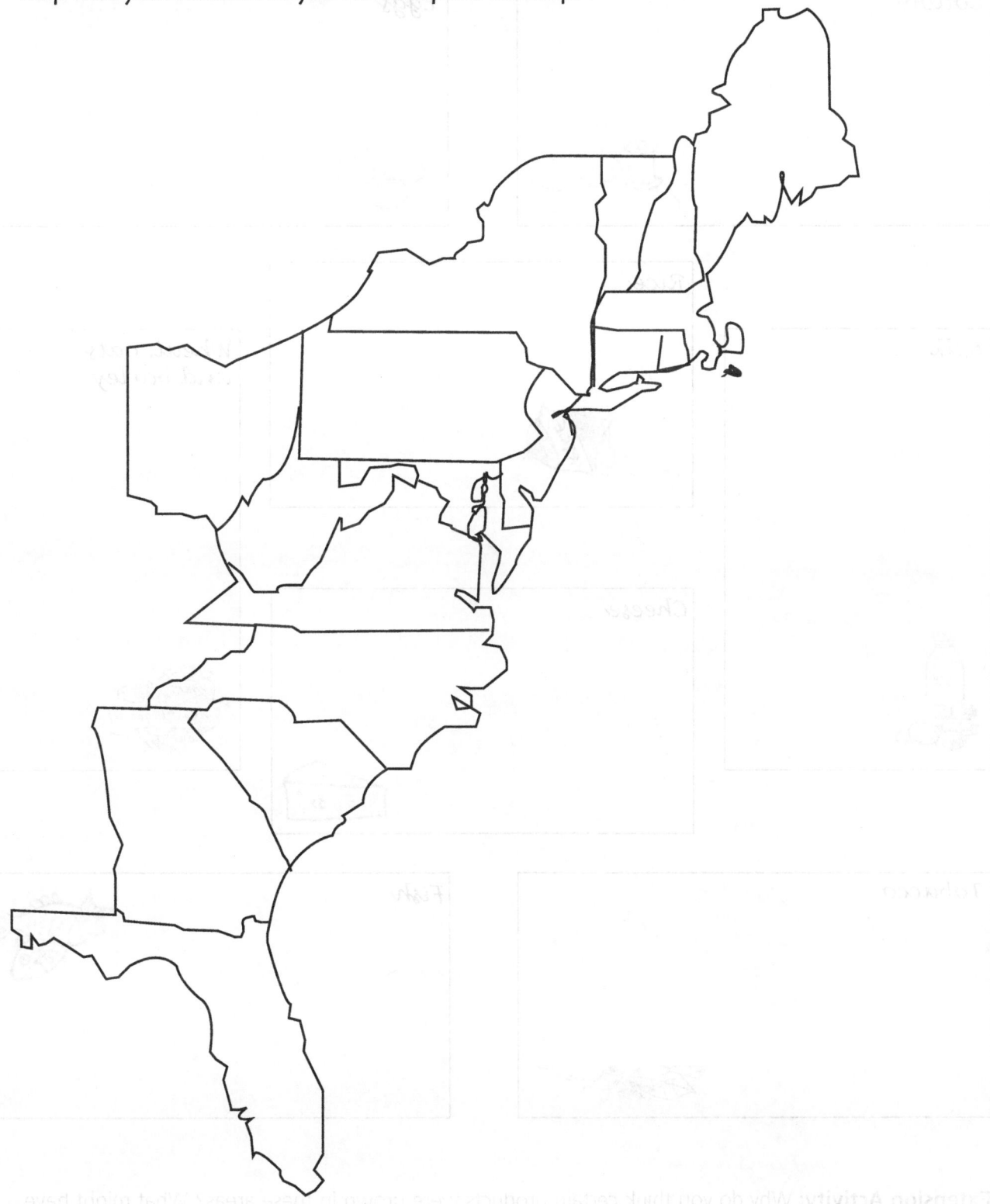

Extension Activity: Conduct research using the Internet about New England and see if you can find out if any other evidence of the original settlers remains today.

What did your new land grow?

☞ By the time the east coast of North America had become the thirteen colonies many goods were being grown for both the settlers' own purposes and for trading with other countries. For the following goods and crops say where they were produced.

Extension Activity: Why do you think certain products were grown in these areas? What might have influenced what people grew and where they grew it? Are the same products still produced in these areas today?

Depth Study: British America

The *Mayflower*

☞ One of the most famous ships to sail to America was the *Mayflower*. Complete the following fact file sheet about this famous ship.

When did the *Mayflower* reach America?
_____
_____
_____
_____
_____

Who was on board?
_____
_____
_____
_____
_____

Why had they come to America?
_____
_____
_____
_____
_____

Depth Study: British America

The triangular trade (1)

The slave trade was a brutal business and was sometimes known as 'the slave triangle,' or 'triangular trade'.

☞ Using the flow chart below explain how the slave triangle worked. There is a word bank to help you for each of the three sections.

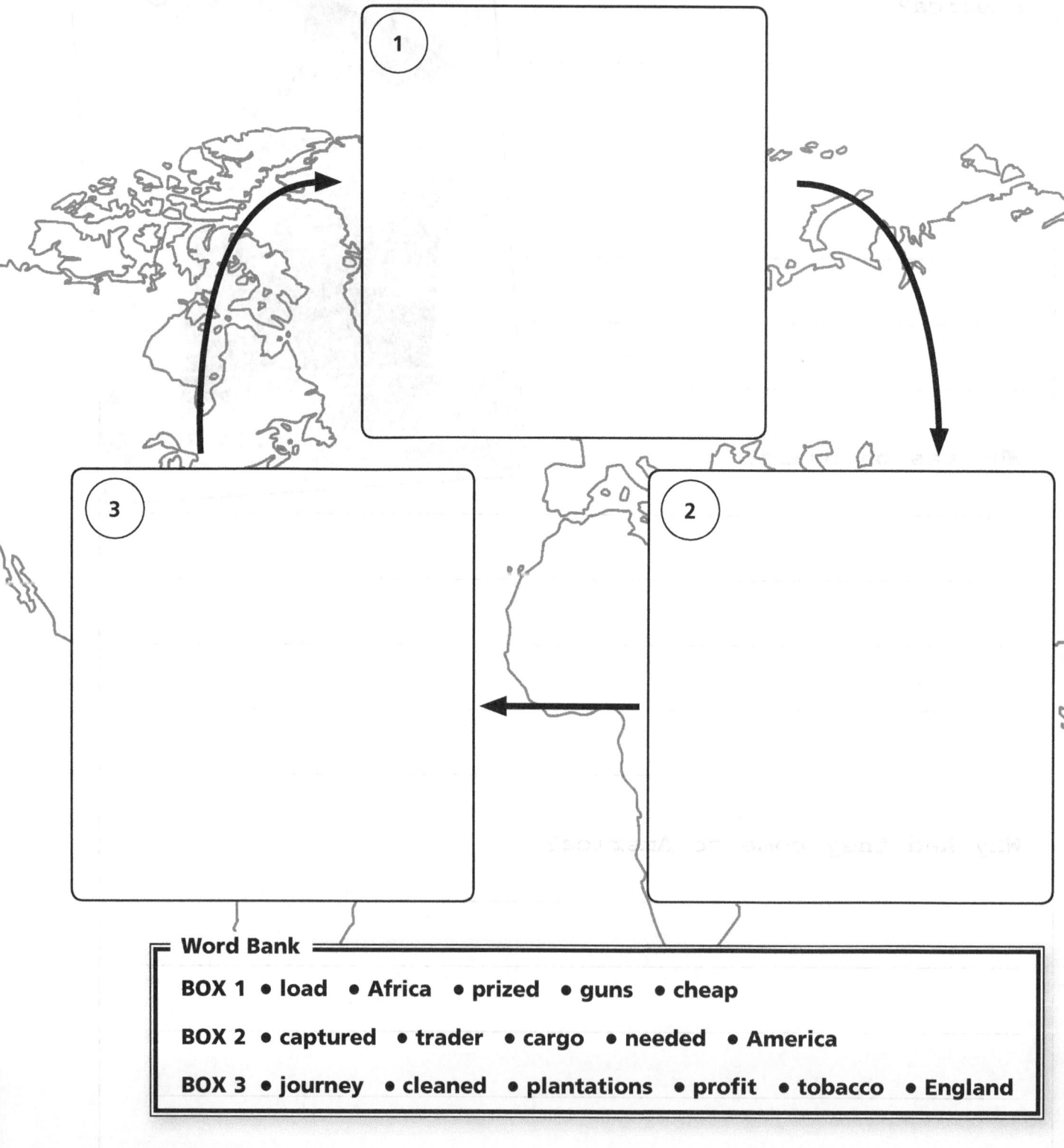

Word Bank

BOX 1 • load • Africa • prized • guns • cheap

BOX 2 • captured • trader • cargo • needed • America

BOX 3 • journey • cleaned • plantations • profit • tobacco • England

Depth Study: British America

The triangular trade (2)

The slave trade was a brutal business and was sometimes known as 'the slave triangle,' or 'triangular trade'.

☞ Using the flow chart below explain how the slave triangle worked.

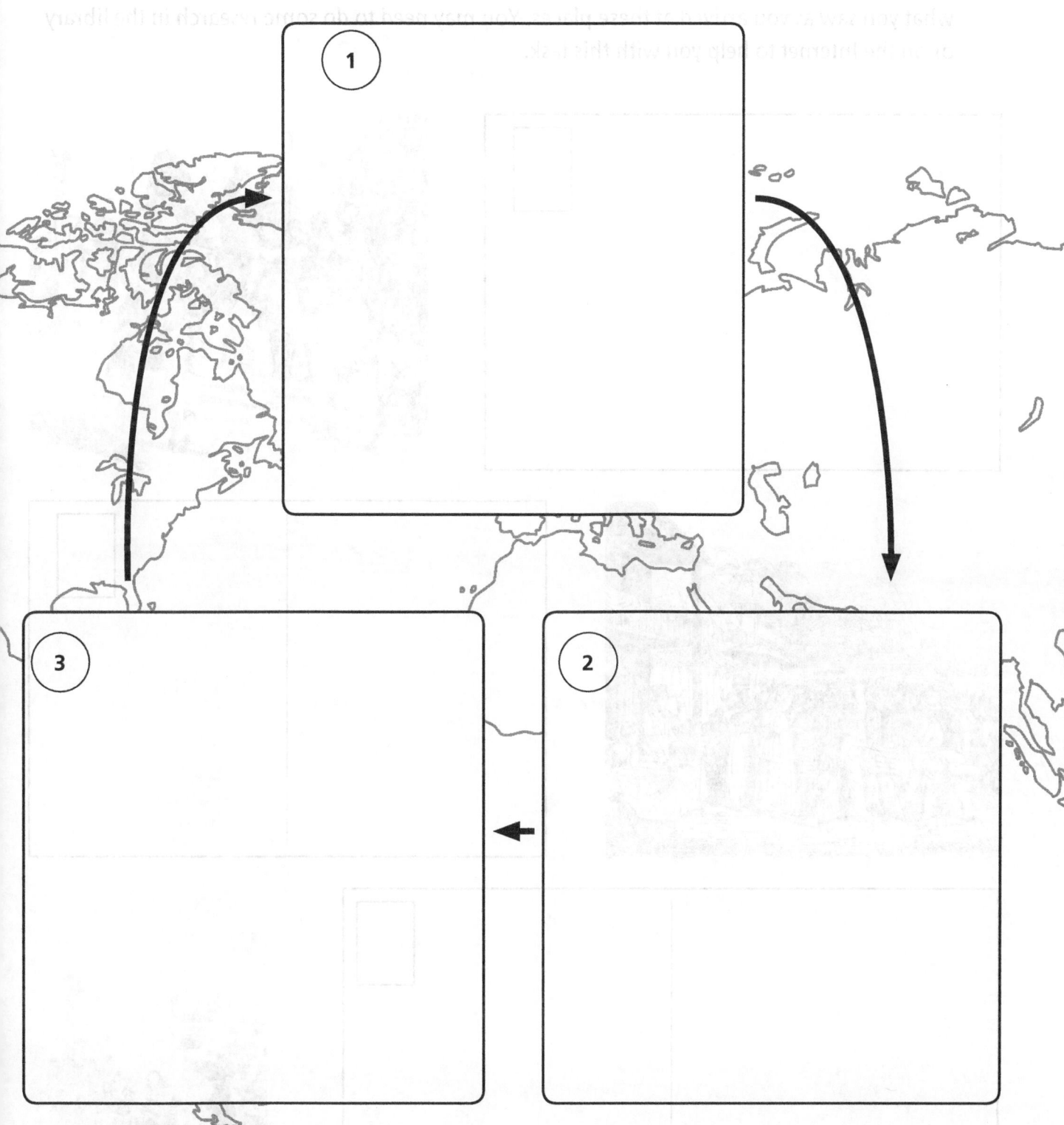

Extension Activity: How long did this journey take? How long was it before a trader saw his ships returning to England after setting sail for Africa? Can you find out about any particular ships that didn't make it?

Every brick in the city of Liverpool

The men responsible for, and involved in, the slave trade must have seen some sights – from loading ships on the docks at Liverpool to exchanging goods for captured slaves on the African coast, the horrific 'Middle Passage' over the Atlantic and the life of slavery waiting in the Americas.

☞ Imagine you are the captain of one of the slave ships. Write three postcards home to explain what you saw as you arrived at these places. You may need to do some research in the library or on the Internet to help you with this task.

Depth Study: British America

© Oxford University Press (copiable page)

The Boston Tea Party

☞ Below are a set of statements which tell the events of 1773 to 1776. Decide which ones are relevant, cut them out and stick them into your workbook in the correct date order.

- Three hundred and forty-two crates full of tea worth over £11,000 were dumped into the sea, right there in Boston harbour.

- Meetings were now held in secret. Fifty-six representatives from the American colonies met to decide what to do… They decided to fight the British.

- Five years later after much fighting and the loss of many lives, Lord Cornwallis of the British Army surrendered.

- Resentment began to grow in America as the British government continued to tax the American settlers.

- The Americans' anger was heightened when the British government ordered the closure of Boston's port and banned all town meetings.

- George Washington was appointed the leader of the army to fight the British soldiers.

- The first ever flag of the USA was made up of 13 stars and 13 stripes to symbolize the 13 colonies.

- The British government decided to place a tax on a cup of tea! Three pence of every pound spent on tea was paid in tax.

- Angered, the British sent soldiers to sort out the American rebels and force them to stay loyal.

- Congress met again, this time formally declaring themselves independent from Britain.

- The Americans were not happy at all! They dressed as Native Americans and boarded three ships moored in Boston.

- 4 July is known as Independence Day in America, and is celebrated with a public holiday every year.

Extension Activity: Once you have placed the events in order, write down the relevant dates from this list next to them: 1773, 1774, 1775, 1776, 1781.

Boston times

The Boston Tea Party was big news. The newspapers of the time would have been full of the events of that day in 1773.

☞ Using information from the Student's Book and by conducting further research write a newspaper article to tell the American public what happened.

Remember, this is an American newspaper so your article will have an American bias! Try to include the following words in your article: taxes, protest, Boston Harbour, anger, natives, freedom.

The Boston Times

1773

There was an old lady lived over the sea

☞ The American song below tells the story of the Boston Tea Party. Read through it, and as you do so, annotate it to explain what you think it means: some lines are a little less obvious than others.

There was an old lady lived over the sea
And she was an Island Queen.
Her daughter lived off in a new countrie,
With an ocean of water between.
The old lady's pockets were full of gold
But never contented was she,
So she called on her daughter to pay her a tax
Of three pence a pound on her tea.
'Now mother, dear mother,' the daughter replied,
'I shan't do the thing you ax.
I'm willing to pay a fair price for the tea,
But never the three penny tax.'
'You shall,' quoth the mother, and reddened with rage,
'For you're my own daughter, you see,
And sure, 'tis quite proper the daughter should pay
Her mother a tax on her tea.'
And so the old lady her servant called up
And packed off a budget of tea,
And eager for three pence a pound, she put
In enough for a large family.
She order'd her servants to bring home the tax,
Declaring her child should obey,
Or old as she was, and almost woman grown,
She'd half whip her life away.
The tea was conveyed to the daughter's door,
All down by the ocean's side,
And the bouncing girl pour'd out every pound
In the dark and boiling tide.
And then she called out to the Island Queen,
'O mother, dear mother,' quoth she,
'Your tea you may have when 'tis steep'd enough
But never a tax from me.'

Extension Activity: Write your own poem or song about the events that took place in 1773.

Independence!

Fifty-six people signed the Declaration of Independence. You can see their signatures below.

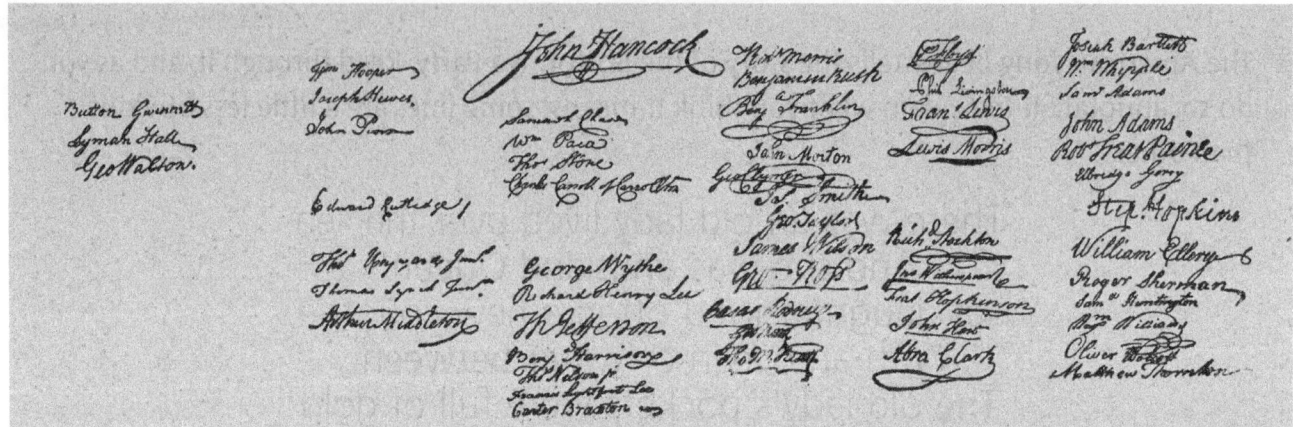

☞ The following are some of the names that can be found on this important document. See what you can find out about each of them. What contribution did they make to the way in which America's history was changed forever?

| John Hancock | Thomas Jefferson | Benjamin Franklin | John Adams | Edward Rutledge |

_____
_____
_____
_____
_____
_____
_____
_____
_____
_____
_____
_____

Extension Activity: The Declaration of Independence is a very interesting document indeed. Use the Internet or the library to research what the document said. Don't just copy down a translation of the words, try to interpret their meaning; perhaps write out what the declaration says in your own words.

America wordsearch

☞ The following words about the birth of America can be found in the wordsearch below. Look carefully to see if you can find them all. When you have completed the wordsearch write a definition for each of the words.

Word Bank

- Columbus • Planters • Slave • Revolution • Jamestown • Colonies
- Plantations • Boston Tea Party • Virginia • New World • John Hawkins
- Settler • Tobacco • *Mayflower* • Trash gangs • Congress

B	C	E	U	Z	P	L	A	N	T	E	R	S	O	F
O	C	O	N	G	R	E	S	S	Q	J	E	G	E	J
S	J	J	L	A	Y	P	E	U	D	O	W	N	Y	G
T	A	S	D	O	A	F	T	D	M	H	J	A	B	N
O	M	N	Q	V	N	O	T	O	I	N	I	G	P	B
N	E	O	U	I	E	I	L	F	X	H	V	H	N	G
T	S	I	W	C	W	K	E	T	P	A	B	S	O	V
E	T	T	A	N	W	H	R	S	T	W	G	A	I	I
A	O	A	T	L	O	K	T	L	I	K	H	R	T	R
P	W	T	O	Z	R	N	C	A	E	I	C	T	U	G
A	N	N	B	V	L	H	B	V	M	N	J	S	L	I
R	C	A	A	R	D	G	L	E	Y	S	X	K	O	N
T	M	L	C	O	L	U	M	B	U	S	R	K	V	I
Y	D	P	C	Q	S	A	Z	S	L	L	H	X	E	A
F	M	R	O	M	A	Y	F	L	O	W	E	R	R	W

© Oxford University Press (copiable page)

Depth Study: British America

The American story

Complete the following fact file. There are also fact files on India and Australia so you can consider the similarities and differences between these parts of the British Empire from the time early settlers arrived to the events that formed history.

FACT FILE: The American Story

When was America discovered? _____

_____

How was it discovered? _____

_____

By whom? _____

_____

What happened as the British arrived?

What was it like for the early settlers?

What did America have to offer the British?

What interesting facts have you learnt?

Olaudah Equiano

☞ Olaudah Equiano was an important figure in history. His best-selling book about his life story helped to turn people against slavery. Use the Internet and the library to find out more information about him so you can complete the fact file below. Include an image of Equiano – you could even draw his portrait!

FACT FILE: Olaudah Equiano

Born: _____

Died: _____

Occupation: _____

Marital status: _____

Children: _____

Early life (where did he grow up? Did anything important happen to him or his family?):
_____
_____
_____
_____
_____

How did he become a slave? _____
_____
_____
_____
_____

When was he freed? _____

What did his book say? _____
_____
_____

Why did it cause such controversy? _____
_____
_____
_____

The Big Question: Should Britain make up for its role in slavery?

Slavery sucks

The source below shows how many slaves could be packed onto the slave ship *Brookes*. This image, and others like it, were used on anti-slavery posters to demonstrate the terrors of the slave trade. Using this source as inspiration, produce your own anti-slavery poster, pamphlet or leaflet.

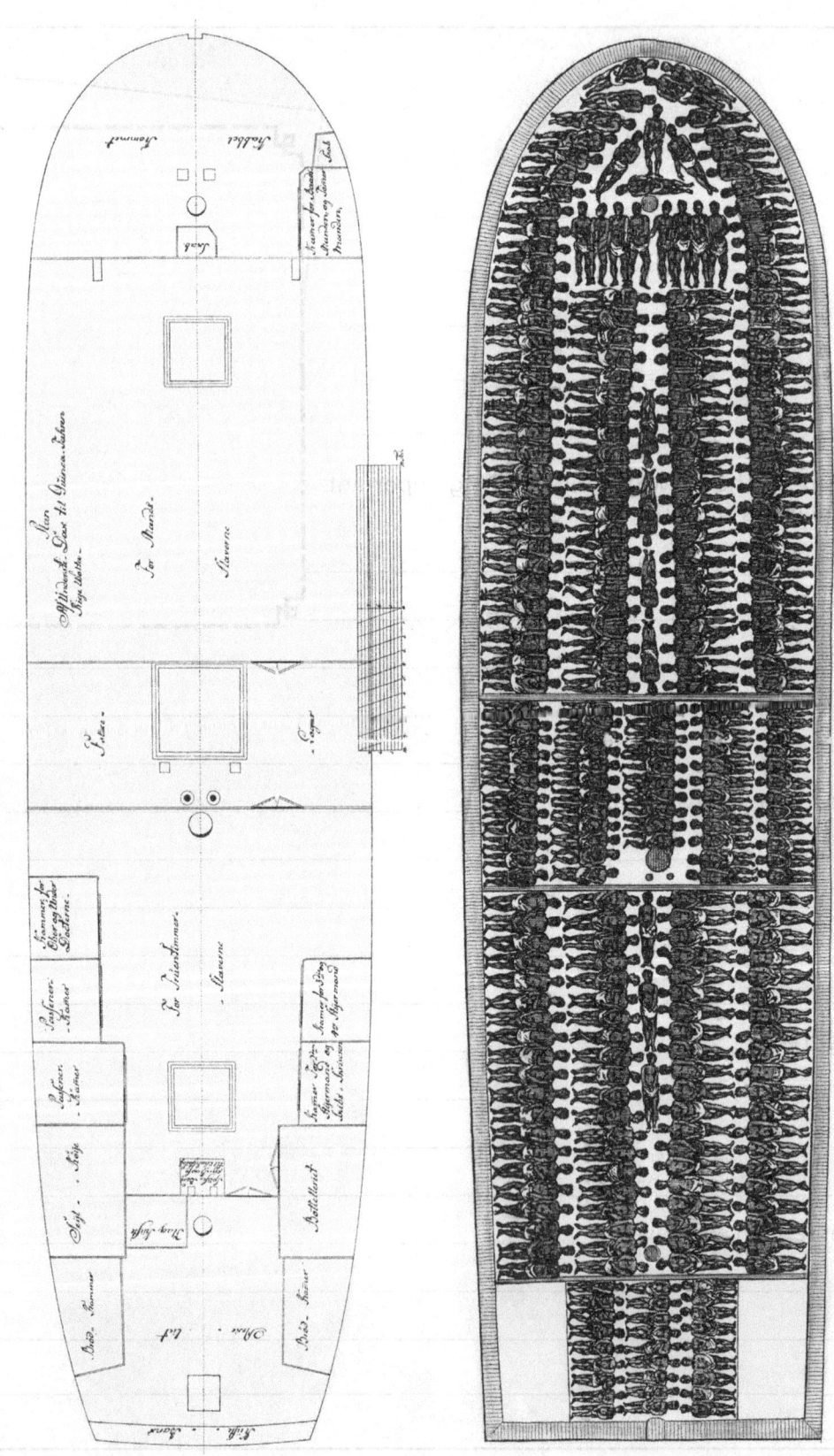

Slavery divides Europe

The following headline highlights how arguments were rife at a UN racism summit in September 2001 about whether European Union countries should apologize for the transatlantic slave trade.

☞ Using what you have learnt about different countries' roles in the slave trade, and through Internet research about the UN racism summit, complete the following article. Use the Word Bank to help you.

Word Bank
- Spain • Portugal • Humanity • Belgium
- Regret • Compensation • Debate • Politicians

SLAVERY ROW DIVIDES EUROPE

Divisions have emerged among European Union countries on whether to apologize for the transatlantic slave trade at a UN racism summit…

_____
_____
_____
_____
_____
_____
_____
_____
_____
_____
_____
_____
_____
_____
_____
_____
_____
_____
_____
_____

The Big Question: Should Britain make up for its role in slavery?

The compensation debate

☞ Below are a series of opinions about whether Britain should pay compensation to African nations for the slave trade. Using the following headings, write out the different opinions in your own words in your workbook and then colour code them: those in favour of compensation should be in red and those against should be in blue.

Headings
- Racism • Compensation from taxes • Africa • But Britain stopped it!
- Criminals! • Where does it end? • Family • Help for ancestors

"Slavery was racist – it depended on the belief that white people were better than other races. That belief is wrong – plain and simple! People should never have been allowed to own others... what about human rights? Aren't we all created equal?"

"The countries that made money out of slavery should help the ancestors of those slaves in Africa today. It doesn't have to be money – but perhaps they could provide education, medical care, irrigation schemes and so on."

"The compensation would have to come out of taxes, paid for by the British public. Is it really fair for people in modern Britain to pay for something that happened so long ago? People today shouldn't be made to feel guilty about something that a different generation did!"

"Where would it end? Should Denmark pay compensation to Britain for attacks by the Vikings? Or the Queen to Catholics for the closing of the Catholic monasteries by Henry VIII? No one is left alive today who made money out of slavery – or who personally suffered from it!"

"The slave trade destroyed Africa. The traders took the young, strong Africans – and left the old, weak and sick. Africa never recovered! Slavery helped make Britain rich – at the expense of Africa. Britain owes Africa for this!"

"The slaves were treated so badly – families were ripped apart and African villages were devastated. Surely someone must pay for that!"

"Loads of other countries were involved in the slave trade too – but Britain stopped slavery first, and then spent the next 100 years trying to get other countries to stop!"

"Many of the slaves were criminals in their own tribes – sold into slavery by their tribal leaders. So it wasn't just whites who were involved in the slave trade."

The Big Question: Should Britain make up for its role in slavery?

A British response: what would you say?

In 2001 British politicians were asked repeatedly for their thoughts and opinions on slavery, but they refused to apologize. Instead they said that they expressed regret about the slave trade.

☞ After studying Britain's role in the slave trade and having listened to different people's opinions, imagine you are a British politician and write your own speech. What would you say? Would you apologize? Would you admit your country's guilt? Use the Word Bank to help you.

_____
_____
_____
_____
_____
_____
_____
_____
_____
_____
_____
_____
_____

Word Bank

- Compensation • Crime • Abolition • Debate • Humanity

Once upon a time...

The true story of the Taj Mahal is one of sadness and romance. It is a symbol of the Muslim faith and is what many people today think of when they think of India.

☞ Research the story of the Taj Mahal. Then write a story to help explain the existence of it. Your story should include why it was built and some information about who built it. You should also include what happened to the family members of the people who built the Taj Mahal after it was finished. Your story should be aimed at Year 6 students to read during their history lesson.

A divided nation

Three of the world's major religions – Hinduism, Buddhism and Sikhism – originated in India.

☞ Some of the beautiful temples built to represent each of these faiths are shown below. Research each of these religions to find out which parts of India they could be found in and the influence they had on India during the time leading up to the country becoming part of the British Empire.

Hinduism

_____
_____
_____
_____

Buddhism

_____
_____
_____
_____
_____
_____
_____
_____
_____

Sikhism

_____
_____
_____
_____
_____
_____
_____

Conquest

Many people have tried to conquer India, visiting it either to make trade links (to make them rich) or to try to take over completely.

☞ Which of the following people or nations came first? Find out when each of the following visited India, then list them in order around the map, starting with number 1.

Headings
- The Persians
- Genghis Khan
- The Chinese
- The French
- The Iranians
- Alexander the Great
- The Dutch
- The British

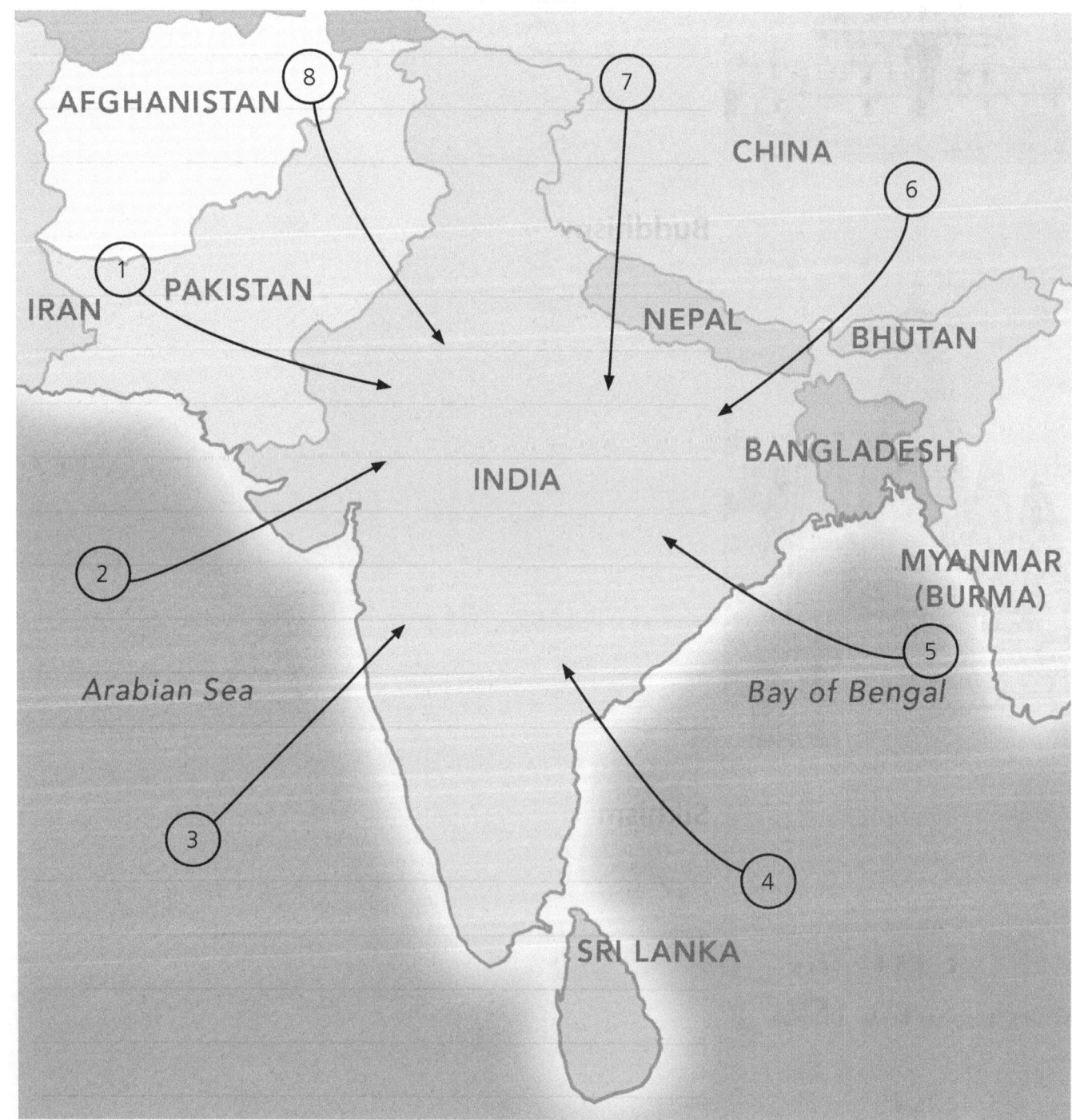

Depth Study: India

How to make a fortune from trade

☞ British trading stations in India were all run by one company; but how did they make their money? Write out captions for each of the following cartoons to explain how the East India Company became so successful.

Who owned what?

With permission from the local Indian rulers, traders began to set up permanent trading stations. British trading stations in India were all run by one company, but how did they make their money? Write our captions for each of the following cartoons to explain how the East India Company became so successful.

✍ Using the map below complete the key to show which country owned each of the ports shown. Then, using the Internet, research when each of the trading ports was established and write the date next to each of the ports on the map.

✍ Which country owned the most trading ports? Can you see a pattern? Conduct some further research into which goods were traded at some of the ports: were some trading ports more successful than others?

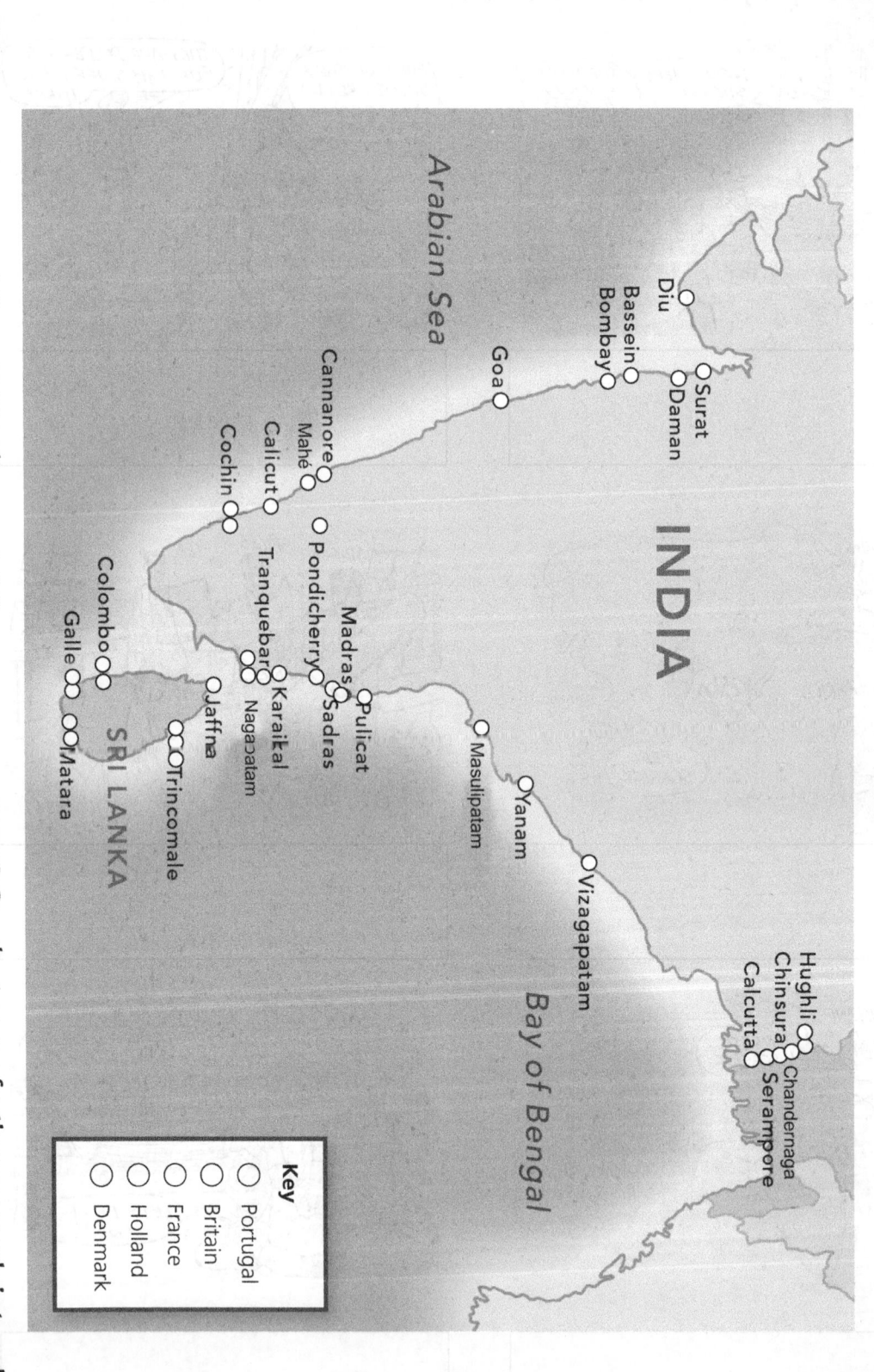

Key
- ○ Portugal
- ○ Britain
- ○ France
- ○ Holland
- ○ Denmark

44 Depth Study: India   © Oxford University Press (copiable page)

The Battle of Plassey

The Battle of Plassey was a very important battle for the East India Company – but why?

☞ Read the statements below. Cut out the statements and arrange them into the correct order to work out why this battle was so important. Number them and stick them into your workbook.

After a brief (but fierce) battle, Fort William surrendered. Only 146 Europeans survived the fight.

The British trading post was called Fort William and was run by the East India Company. The man in charge of Fort William (the governor) also gave shelter to one of Siraj's relatives who had fallen out with him.

The land around the trading posts was ruled by Siraj-ud-Daulah. It was a rich area of land and Siraj preferred to do business with the French.

On 23 June 1957 the two sides met up near a village called Plassey and faced each other to fight. Siraj had 60,000 troops and was supported by French cannons.

Siraj wasn't happy – he demanded the release of his relative (so he could be executed). The governor refused, so Siraj got an army together to attack Fort William.

Whilst waiting for the battle to start the British sheltered in a wood under the trees. Suddenly a violent thunderstorm started and rain soaked the whole area.

After the storm, Siraj's men charged at the British, but their guns were useless. The British met the charging Indians with devastating gunfire.

In the 1750s the British and French set up large trading posts near Calcutta in Northern India.

The small room in which the prisoners were kept was known as the 'black hole of Calcutta'. When news of the incident reached Britain, people were horrified. Many said that Siraj should be punished.

The survivors were locked in a cell only six metres by six metres. Without water and struggling for air, many died. When the door was opened in the morning 123 of the prisoners had been suffocated and trampled to death.

Siraj's men and more importantly their gunpowder got very wet. Gunpowder won't work properly if it gets wet. Clive's troops on the other hand were sheltered under the trees.

Siraj fled the battlefield on a horse and the Indians were beaten. The British had removed the most powerful Indian in Bengal and now ran this rich part of India themselves.

A few weeks later a British army colonel working in India for the East Indian Company was ordered to deal with Siraj. His name was Robert Clive and he had around 3000 troops under his command.

The governor of Fort William, together with the women and children, ran away, leaving about 900 Europeans left to fight Siraj's army of 50,000.

Extension Activity: Now try writing a report to the people in charge of the East India Company back home in Britain telling them of the events of 1757. Remember, it would be a British male who would be reporting back!

Life as a Sepoy

☞ This picture shows a Sepoy – a local Indian recruited by the British Army as a soldier – but what was life like for him and thousands of others? What do you think an Indian Sepoy would write in his journal about what his daily life was like? What would he say about the way he was treated by the British and about the equipment they were expected to use? How might the way they felt about their jobs have led to the mutiny of 1857? Consider these questions and then complete this Indian soldier's journal entry below.

It has been two months since I became a Sepoy…

46 Depth Study: India

Remember Cawnpore

Below is a story about one of the most famous battles of the Sepoy revolution that happened at a place called Cawnpore.

☞ Read the statements below. Cut out the statements and arrange them into the correct order of what happened at Cawnpore. Number them and stick them into your workbook.

The British dug trenches and re-enforced the walls of a small camp they had built in preparation for the attack. The camp also had a well for water.

On the morning of the 27 June the British left Cawnpore. They were marched to a riverbank where there were boats to take them down river to safety. All the Indian rebels had turned out to see them go.

Instead, some local butchers were hired to kill the women and children. They battered down the doors and slaughtered them with meat cleavers.

The attacks continued after Nana Sahib's arrival. By now disease had broken out in the British camp and they were short of food, water and medicine.

Whilst getting into the boats, someone fired a shot. To this day historians don't know who fired at who first. However, soon both sides were firing at each other. Hundreds of Britons were killed in the gun battle: some of those trying to get out of the water were cut down by the Indian cavalry.

News of the Sepoy rebellion soon spread all over India.

In the town of Cawnpore the British who lived there prepared for an attack. There were 900 people in total, but only 300 were in the army. The rest were mainly women, children and servants.

The following morning the bodies were collected up, some still alive, and thrown down the local well.

Most of the Indians under Sahib's command refused to shoot at women and children. Some even fired their rifles in the air when ordered to shoot at them in Bibighar house.

The 120 or so women and children who had survived were taken back to Cawnpore and kept in Bibighar house.

Soon after sunrise, a local prince called Nana Sahib arrived. He was angry with the British because they had failed to give him titles, privileges and a pension when his father (another Indian prince) had died. The British argued that he should not get the titles and money because he was an adopted son.

Women and children remained imprisoned for several days. Then news got back to Nana Sahib that British troops were on their way to Cawnpore to fight the Indians. Sahib then made the decision to kill the prisoners.

Just a week into the siege, the general in charge of the British camp heard some devastating news – his son's head had been blown off by a shell. When Nana Sahib asked the general if he wanted to leave Cawnpore, with the men, women and children he readily agreed.

The attack began on the night of the 5 June 1857. The first stage of the attack lasted until the next morning.

Extension Activity: What effect did the battle of Cawnpore have? Why do you think it was such an important battle? What happened next?

The Queen speaks

☞ The passage below is taken from Queen Victoria's proclamation (an official letter) to India in November 1858. It is quite difficult to read but it is very important. Read it carefully and try to answer the questions in your workbook.

> We know, and respect, the feelings of attachment with which the natives of India regard the lands inherited by them from their ancestors, and we desire to protect them in all rights connected therewith, subject to the equitable demands of the State; and we will that generally, in framing and administering the law, due regard be paid to the ancient rights, usages, and customs of India.
>
> Our clemency will be extended to all offenders, save and except those who have been, or shall be, convicted of having directly taken part in the murder of British subjects. With regard to such the demands of justice forbid the exercise of mercy.
>
> When, by the blessing of Providence, internal tranquillity shall be restored, it is our earnest desire to stimulate the peaceful industry of India, to promote works of public utility and improvement, and to administer the government for the benefit of all our subjects resident therein. In their prosperity will be our strength, in their contentment our security, and in their gratitude our best reward. And may the God of all power grant to us, and to those in authority under us, strength to carry out these our wishes for the good of our people.

1. What does the Queen say to try and reassure the people of India?
2. How does she suggest that the British will respect the traditional way of life in India?
3. What does the Queen promise all those who have been in trouble with the law?
4. Who does she say she can't make this promise to?
5. List three things the Queen says she hopes will happen in India once peace has been restored.
6. How does the last paragraph make you feel? Do you think she is being fair to the people of India? If not, why not?

Extension Activity: Find out about what else this proclamation says. You will find a copy of this famous letter either in your local library or on the Internet.

Who was Curzon?

George Nathaniel Curzon was a very important figure in both India and Britain's history, but what did he do? Who was he? And what role did he play in British history?

☞ Complete the curriculum vitae below to find out more about this important man. You will need to use the library and the Internet to help you.

Name:

Born:

Birthplace:

Family details:

Job titles (with dates):

What role was he given in 1898?

What changes did he make in India? (Were they all seen as successful? Study source G on page 35 of the Student's Book to help you.)

Why did he resign his post?

Which political party did he belong to?

What other important roles did he have after he resigned?

When and where did he die?

Extension Activity: Draw a timeline of Curzon's life. He lived during some important times in British history, but *when* did he play an important role and what did he do?

© Oxford University Press (copiable page)   Depth Study: India   49

I write on behalf of...

☞ Study the image below and the quote from Florence Nightingale. What do they tell you about the Indian famine of the late 1800s? Using the sources and further research to help you, write a letter on behalf of Florence Nightingale to the Queen of England explaining what she means in her statement. Think carefully about what you would tell the Queen about the way Indian people are being treated and how they are forced to live.

You might want to include the following ideas:
- The main causes of the famine.
- The number of people affected.
- The impact it is having on the lives of the people of India.
- How the behaviour of the British and their policies have made matters worse.
- What you believe should be done.

Source 1

Source 2

Approximately six million Indians died because of the Indian famine of the late 1800s, and many blamed the British for not doing enough. Even Florence Nightingale, the famous British nurse, said 'We do not care enough to stop them dying slow and terrible deaths from things we could easily stop. We have taken their land, and we rule it, for our good, not theirs'.

What impact?

☞ Complete this Venn diagram to help you understand both the positive and negative impact of British rule over India. The area in the middle is for the ideas you have where you could argue both positive and negative effects of British rule.

Think about your answers carefully and remember to explain your reasons. An example has been provided to help you.

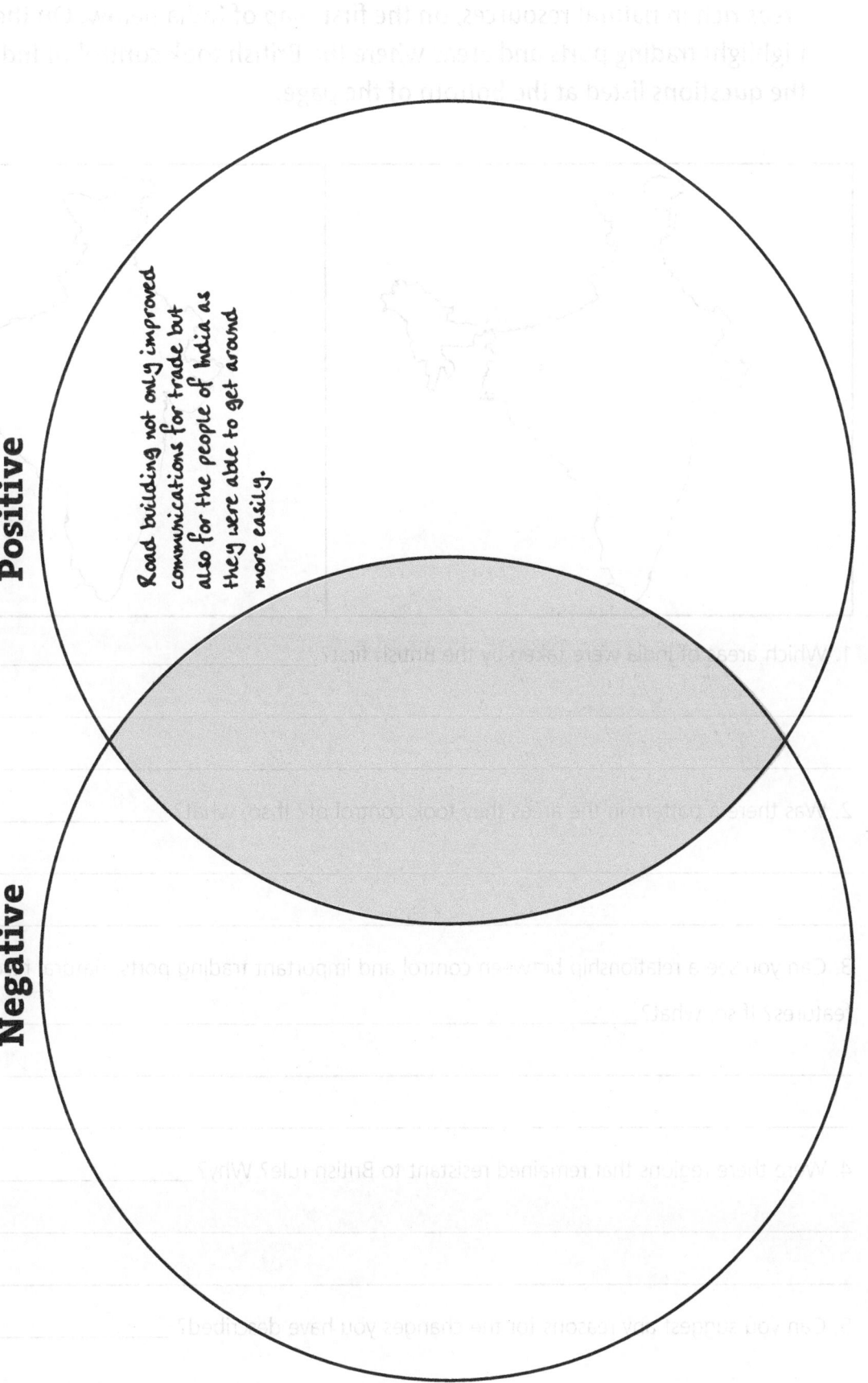

Positive

Road building not only improved communications for trade but also for the people of India as they were able to get around more easily.

Negative

© Oxford University Press (copiable page)

Depth Study: India 51

The growth of Britain's control over India

☞ Using an atlas, highlight major physical features such as mountain ranges, rivers and areas rich in natural resources, on the first map of India below. On the second map highlight trading ports and areas where the British took control of India. Then answer the questions listed at the bottom of the page.

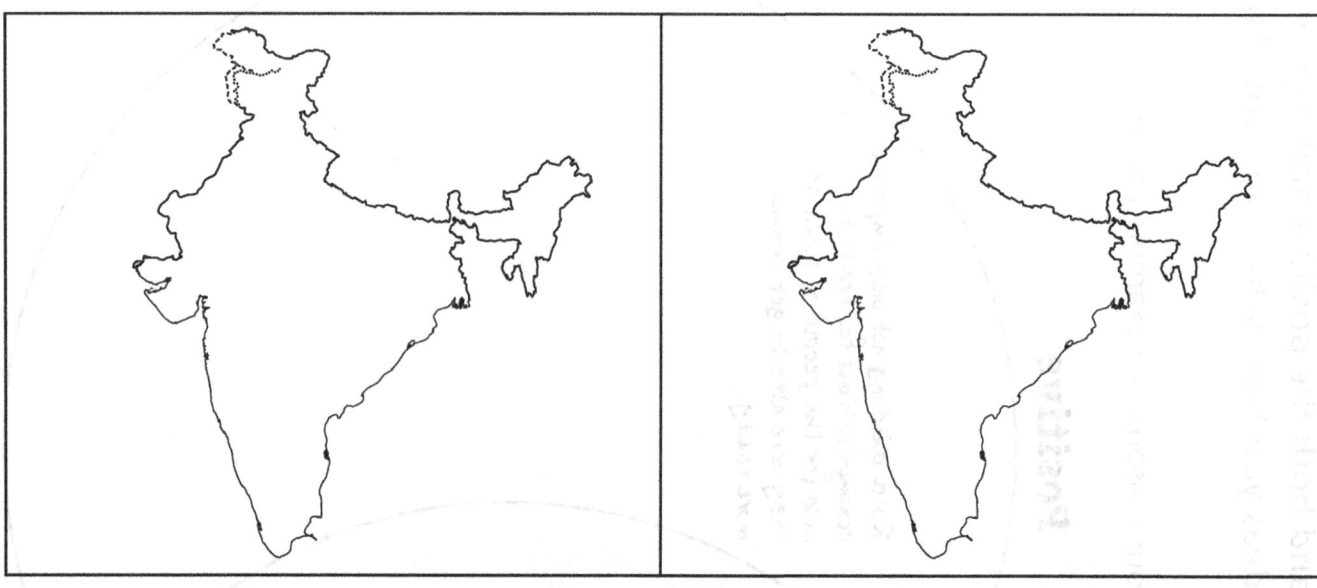

1. Which areas of India were taken by the British first? _____
_____
_____

2. Was there a pattern in the areas they took control of? If so, what? _____
_____
_____

3. Can you see a relationship between control and important trading ports, natural resources and physical features? If so, what? _____
_____
_____

4. Were there regions that remained resistant to British rule? Why? _____
_____
_____

5. Can you suggest any reasons for the changes you have described? _____
_____

The salt tax

☞ Using what you already know about the salt tax and Gandhi's 'satyagraha', and by conducting further research using the Internet, produce a propaganda poster encouraging people to protest against the salt tax.

Ensure your poster explains what the salt tax is and why people should join the protest. Explain the kind of person you are looking for and what you want them to do if they join you. Include pictures to make your poster more attention-grabbing!

Obituary

An obituary is an article or short notice that gives an account of the life of someone who was considered significant. An obituary usually appears in a newspaper shortly after a person has died and summarizes certain information about that person's life and achievements.

☞ Pictured here is Mohandas Gandhi. With the help of research, write an obituary for Gandhi. You must make sure you include a little bit about his family background, his lifetime achievements and what he will be remembered for.

Whose burden?

The White Man's Burden by Rudyard Kipling

Take up the White Man's burden--
Send forth the best ye breed--
Go bind your sons to exile
To serve your captives' need;
To wait in heavy harness,
On fluttered folk and wild--
Your new-caught, sullen peoples,
Half-devil and half-child.

Take up the White Man's burden--
In patience to abide,
To veil the threat of terror
And check the show of pride;
By open speech and simple,
An hundred times made plain
To seek another's profit,
And work another's gain.

Take up the White Man's burden--
No tawdry rule of kings,
But toil of serf and sweeper--
The tale of common things.
The ports ye shall not enter,
The roads ye shall not tread,
Go mark them with your living,
And mark them with your dead.

Take up the White Man's burden--
And reap his old reward:
The blame of those ye better,
The hate of those ye guard--
The cry of hosts ye humour
(Ah, slowly!) toward the light:--
"Why brought he us from bondage,
Our loved Egyptian night?"

The Brown Man's Burden by Henry Labouchère

Pile on the brown man's burden
To gratify your greed;
Go, clear away the "niggers"
Who progress would impede;
Be very stern, for truly
'Tis useless to be mild
With new-caught, sullen peoples,
Half devil and half child.

Pile on the brown man's burden;
And, if ye rouse his hate,
Meet his old-fashioned reasons
With Maxims up to date.
With shells and dumdum bullets
A hundred times made plain
The brown man's loss must ever
Imply the white man's gain.

Pile on the brown man's burden,
And if his cry be sore,
That surely need not irk you--
Ye've driven slaves before.
Seize on his ports and pastures,
The fields his people tread;
Go make from them your living,
And mark them with his dead.

Pile on the brown man's burden,
And through the world proclaim
That ye are Freedom's agent--
There's no more paying game!
And, should your own past history
Straight in your teeth be thrown,
Retort that independence
Is good for whites alone.

Rudyard Kipling's poem *The White Man's Burden* was published in 1899. Henry Labouchère's poem *The Brown Man's Burden* was published a year later in response to Kipling's poem. Read each poem carefully and then answer the following questions in your workbook.

1. What do you think Kipling was trying to say?

2. Kipling writes some very unpleasant things about people from foreign races: what words does he use to describe them?

3. How does he write about the 'white man' in order to make them seem superior?

4. Do you think Kipling could be considered a racist? Explain your answer.

5. How is *The Brown Man's Burden* different to Kipling's poem?

6. What does Labouchère's poem tell us about the way the Indians were treated?

7. What do you think this writer is trying to say about the British?

Timeline of India's history

☞ Below are a series of events in the history of India, events which led to India's independence. Cut out the boxes and the timeline, stick the timeline on an A4 piece of paper and stick the events next to the correct date.

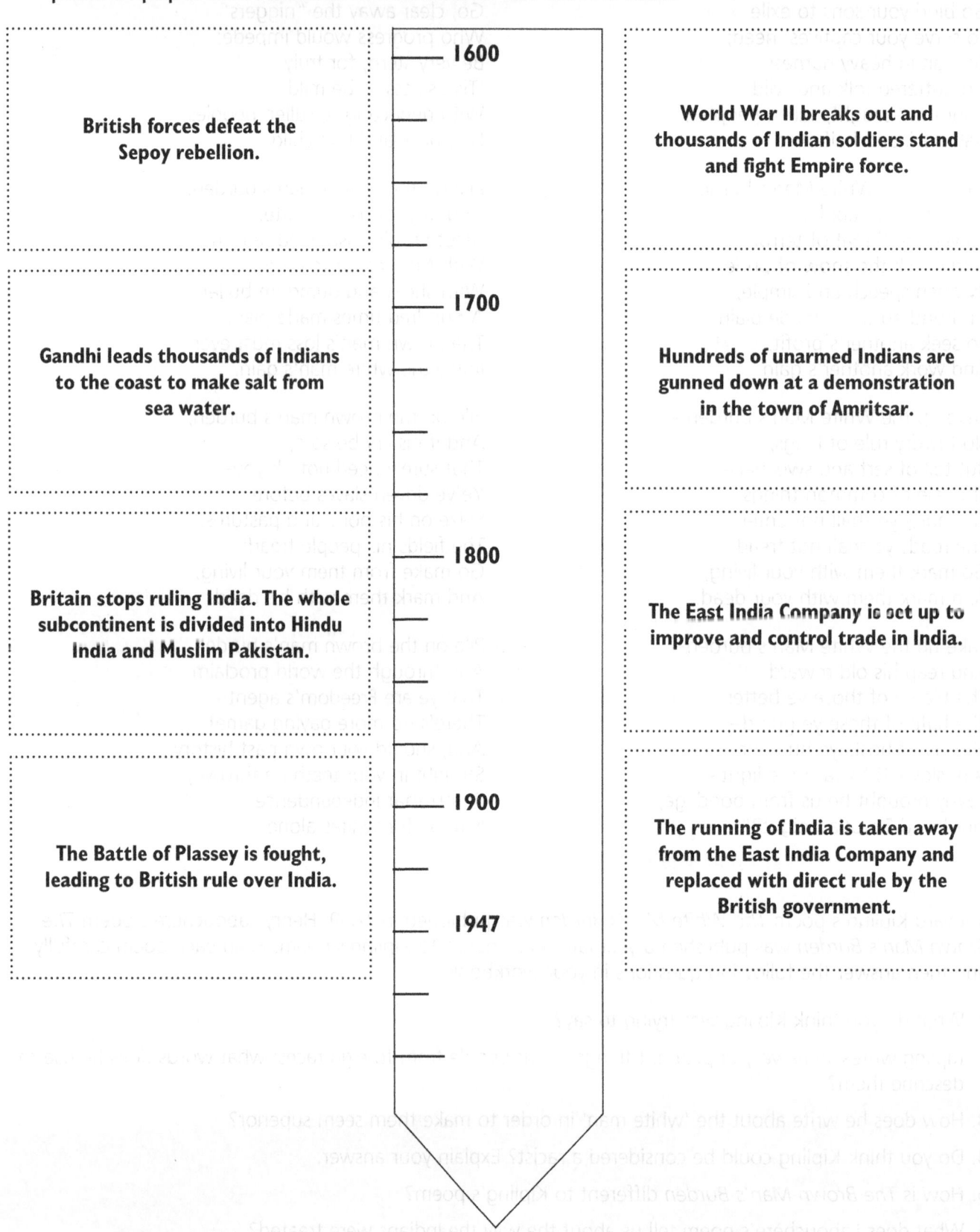

British forces defeat the Sepoy rebellion.

Gandhi leads thousands of Indians to the coast to make salt from sea water.

Britain stops ruling India. The whole subcontinent is divided into Hindu India and Muslim Pakistan.

The Battle of Plassey is fought, leading to British rule over India.

1600

1700

1800

1900

1947

World War II breaks out and thousands of Indian soldiers stand and fight Empire force.

Hundreds of unarmed Indians are gunned down at a demonstration in the town of Amritsar.

The East India Company is set up to improve and control trade in India.

The running of India is taken away from the East India Company and replaced with direct rule by the British government.

56 Depth Study: India © Oxford University Press (copiable page)

India puzzle

☞ Read the clues below and complete the grid by entering your answers.

Clues

1. Ruled Britain from 1837 to 1901.
2. The extreme shortage of food brought on by a long spell of dry weather, which led to crop failure.
3. One of the most famous figures responsible for gaining India its freedom.
4. _____ in the crown.
5. The division in 1947.
6. _____ of India. The name Queen Victoria gave herself.
7. Leader of the Indian political party called the Muslim League.
8. One of the main religions in India.
9. The first Prime Minister of India.
10. Viceroy of India from 1898 to 1905.
11. The name given to the person who was put directly in charge of the country and ran it on behalf of Queen Victoria.
12. Part of the name of the group set up to try and rid India of British control.

☞ Once you have completed the grid you will see that you have created a word down the centre: write a sentence to explain what this word means.

© Oxford University Press (copiable page)   Depth Study: India 57

India word square

☞ Read the following clues and see if you can work out the answers by using the word square grid below – the top letter is the first letter of the answer, the left-hand letter is a letter that appears somewhere in the word and the right-hand letter is the last letter of the answer.

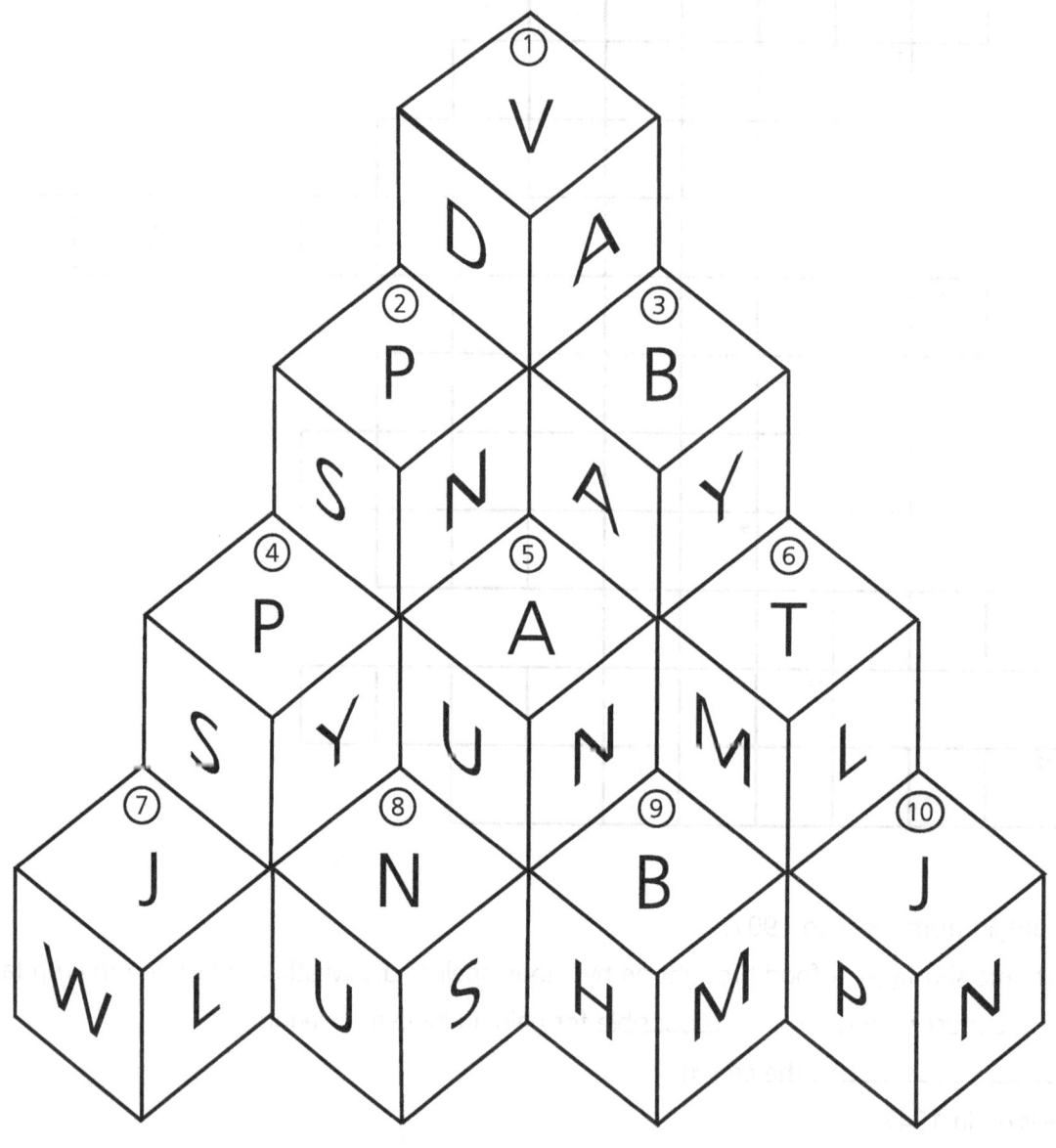

1. Explorer from Portugal who discovered how to get to India by sea: _____
2. This was needed from local Indian rulers in order to set up permanent trading stations: _____
3. The trading post set up in 1668 by the East India Company: _____
4. A victory by the East India Company led by Robert Clive: _____
5. One of the goods loaded onto ships to sell in India: _____
6. Structure built by Shah Jahan. One of India's best-known buildings: _____
7. India was known as the _____ in the crown of Britain's Empire.
8. India was rich in these, including iron ore, copper, gold, silver and gemstones: _____
9. One of the three major religions that originated in India: _____
10. One of the countries British ships travelled to to sell goods they had swapped in India: _____

58   Depth Study: India   © Oxford University Press (copiable page)

India wordsearch

☞ The following words about Indian can be found in the wordsearch below. Look carefully to see if you can find them all. When you have completed the wordsearch write a definition for each of the words.

Word Bank

- Sepoy • Cawnpore • Grease • Colt revolver • Mutiny • Independence
- Lakshmibai • Luxury • Cartridges • Rebellion • Gurkhas • Enfield rifle • Viceroy

C	Q	B	A	L	C	S	I	U	J	Y	P	D	L	T
O	I	N	D	E	P	E	N	D	E	N	C	E	A	G
L	H	R	N	D	B	P	U	G	T	F	E	S	K	E
T	R	A	D	A	V	O	P	N	S	B	L	G	S	Q
R	E	G	W	J	I	Y	H	R	R	X	F	U	H	V
E	M	Y	O	I	C	B	M	B	Y	G	I	R	M	X
V	I	R	E	B	E	L	L	I	O	N	R	K	I	H
O	Q	U	F	S	R	T	P	G	F	Z	D	H	B	E
L	C	X	C	W	O	A	K	R	X	W	L	A	A	R
V	L	U	V	H	Y	F	J	E	N	O	E	S	I	O
E	C	L	L	N	K	I	Y	A	E	J	I	H	R	P
R	P	K	I	A	O	G	R	S	X	V	F	F	Q	N
S	D	T	C	E	U	I	L	E	Z	K	N	M	Y	W
Z	U	P	T	L	W	U	E	V	N	J	E	Z	S	A
M	O	M	E	K	S	E	G	D	I	R	T	R	A	C

© Oxford University Press (copiable page)   Depth Study: India

The Indian story

Complete the following fact file. There are also fact files on America and Australia so you can consider the similarities and differences between these parts of the British Empire from the time early settlers arrived to the events that formed history.

FACT FILE: The Indian Story

When was India discovered? _____

_____

How was it discovered? _____

_____

By whom? _____

_____

What happened as the British arrived?

What was it like for the early settlers?

What did India have to offer the British?

What interesting facts have you learnt?

When did the British take control?

☞ Listed below are the countries under British rule in the 1900s; but when did the British actually take control? Write the following countries onto the appropriate map with details of when the British took control of it.

Word Bank
- Nigeria • Rhodesia • Kenya • India • South Africa • Uganda • Tanganyika
- Burma • Singapore • Hong Kong • Malaya • New Zealand • Canada • Gambia

Map of the British Empire in 1765.

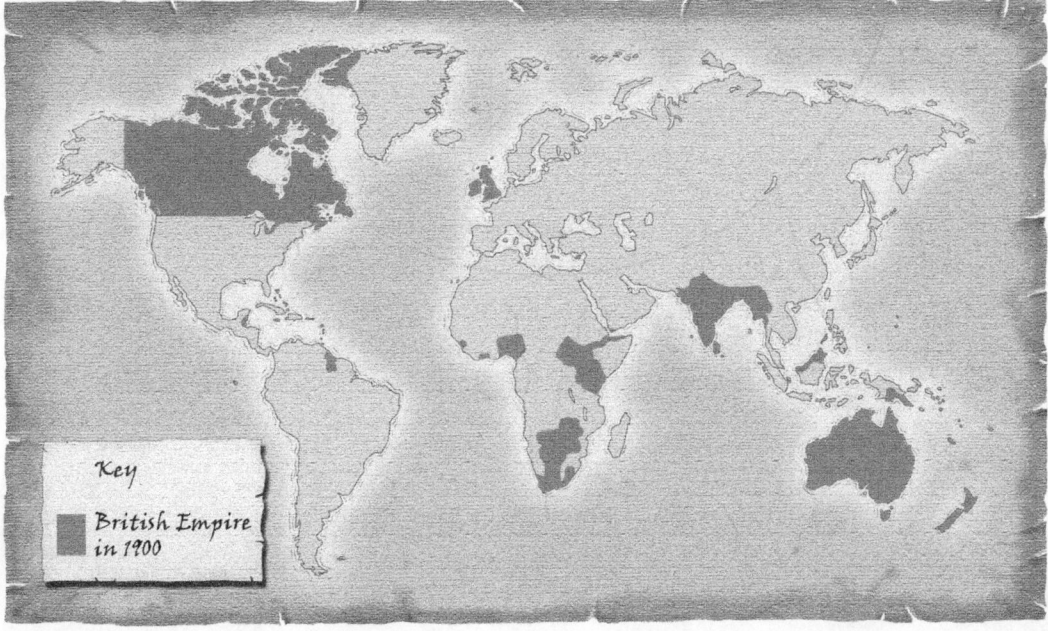

Map of the British Empire in 1900.

Extension Activity: For each of the countries listed find out: the date when the British no longer had control, if they lost control peacefully or through unrest and uprising, and which countries did they keep control of the longest?

The sun never sets

☞ It was often said that the sun never set on the British Empire. Use the diagram below to explain what this phrase meant (you could use Source C on page 43 of the Student's Book as inspiration). Add your own illustrations to represent each of the countries in each time zone and include some historical facts about the British Empire and its control over these places.

Extension Activity: Why was it said that the sun never set on the British Empire?

How did the Empire benefit?

☞ The sources below demonstrate the benefits of the British Empire, but what do they tell us? Annotate the sources to say how you think they provide evidence of the benefits of the British Empire. Use the Word Bank to help you.

Source A: A country house in Gloucestershire.

Source B: Tea from India being unloaded in London.

Source C: Queen Victoria's Diamond Jubilee celebration.

Word Bank

• Style • Buildings • Furniture • Variety • Trade • Transportation

Other benefits

☞ The British Empire wasn't just about making money, there were many other benefits. The sources below summarize what else the Empire did for Britain. Complete the diagram by explaining the benefits of the British Empire: the words you need to include are shown below each heading.

Opportunities abroad
- unemployment • emigrated

Power
- wars • allies

Preventing disease
- cholera • water • bacteria

Pride
- Proud • Rule Britannia
- Commonwealth Games

Buildings
- theatres • cinemas • piers • styles

64 The Big Question: What did the Empire do for Britain?

The life and travels of Cook

☞ James Cook was a very famous explorer, but how much do you know about him? Below are a number of different events in Cook's life – but when did they happen? You will probably need to conduct some research using the library or the Internet. Cut out the events and stick them on a piece of A4 paper in the correct order, remembering to add dates if possible, to tell the story of Cook's life.

Cook's first voyage.	Cook's second voyage.
Aboard his ship *Resolution* Cook set sail in search of the North West Passage.	Cook became an apprentice to a wealthy shipowner called John Walker.
Cook returned to England to marry Elizabeth Batts after travels to survey Canada.	Cook set sail in search of the Antarctic.
Cook arrived at Easter Island.	Cook's ship hit the Great Barrier Reef off the east coast of Australia.
Captain Cook arrived at Hawaii.	Cook met the King and became a member of the Royal Society.
Cook arrived at Botany Bay to collect specimens to take home.	Cook joined the Royal Navy
Born in Marton-in-Cleveland, Yorkshire.	Cook took his third voyage.
Cook was killed in Kealakekua Bay, Hawaii.	Whilst Cook's ship was being repaired many of his crew caught a fever and died.
Cook left Plymouth to lead an expedition to the South Seas. His journey took him to New Zealand.	Cook's ship became the first ever to cross the Antarctic Circle.

Your Royal Highness

☞ Imagine you are one of Cook's shipmates in charge of mapping the new lands you discover on your voyages. After many months at sea you discover New Zealand, and eventually Botany Bay, Australia. On behalf of Cook, write a letter to the King giving information about the new lands you have discovered for the British Empire. Remember, Australia was already inhabited by natives – what will you tell the King about them?

Word Bank
- native tribes
- Christians
- Godless
- Botany Bay
- terror
- terra australis incognita
- claimed
- smallpox

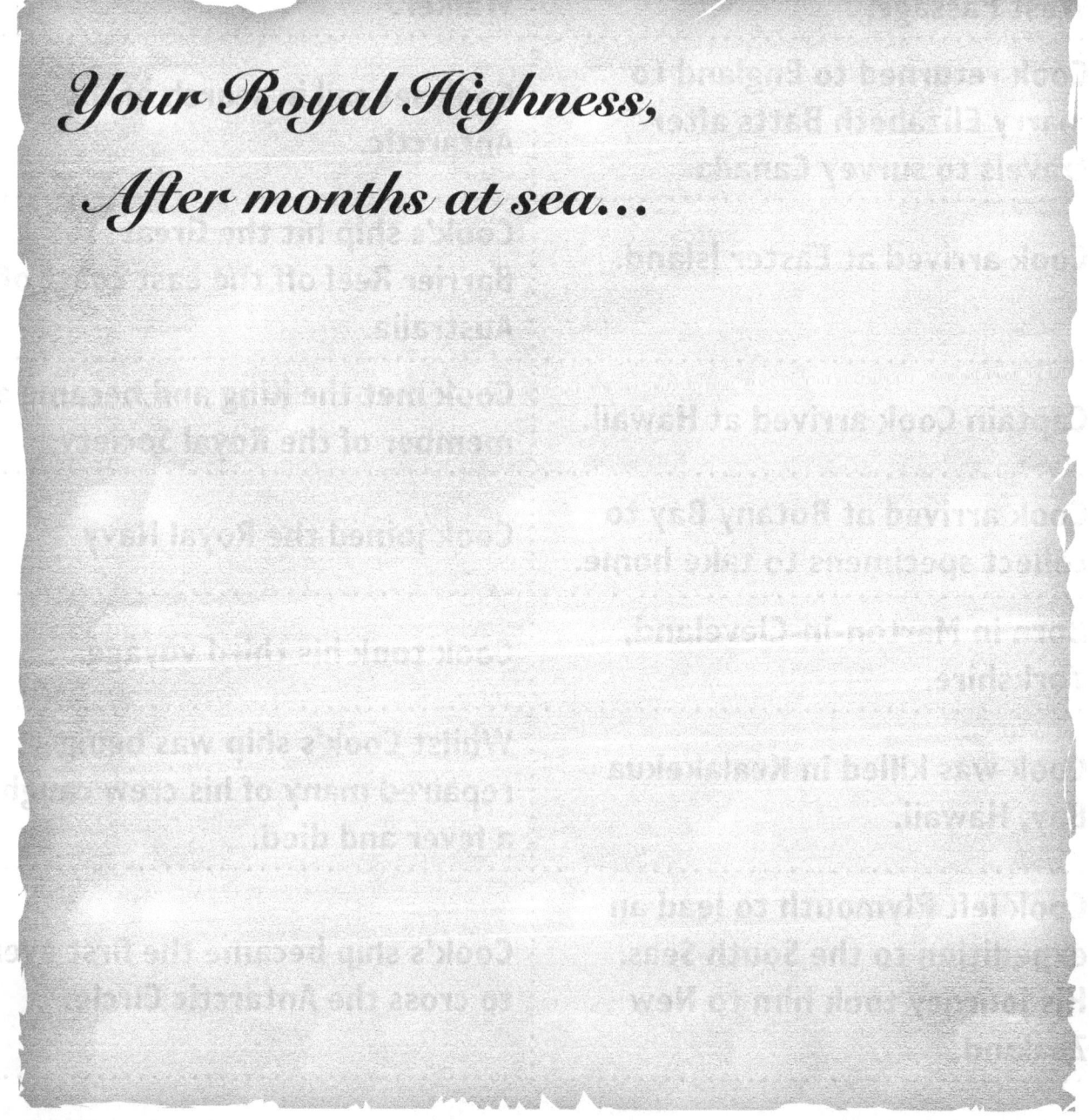

Your Royal Highness,

After months at sea...

Depth Study: A land down under

A little bit of England

Captain Cook was killed on 14 February 1779. This monument was erected to mark where Cook was killed and the area around it was given to the UK.

☞ You have been given the task of writing a plaque to go with this monument to tell visitors about Cook and his contribution to British history. What would you write about his life? The plaque has space for up to 150 words.

Transportation nation

☞ The first ships left for Australia with over 1300 people on board, of which 736 were convicted criminals – so they obviously needed to be kept under control! Using the Internet and the library to help you, write ten rules that the convicts need to follow in order to maintain order during the long voyage. The following link might help you with your research: http://members.iinet.net.au/7perthdps/convicts/shiplife.html.

RULES!

Adventure or invasion?

☞ Below are two inhabitants of Australia with very different points of view. In the speech bubbles suggest what their opinion might be on each of the given topics.

Extension Activity: Who do you agree with and why?

Pemulwuy

Pemulwuy was the leader of a resistance belonging to the Bidjigal nation. He was responsible for carrying out attacks on British settlers and their property, and avoided capture for 12 years!

☞ Using the library and the Internet research who Pemulwuy was and what he did to anger the British. Then design a 'wanted' poster to help capture him and bring him to justice.

The Stolen Generations

In an attempt to strip Aboriginal Australians of their heritage, children were taken from their families, leaving their grief-stricken parents behind. In January 2008 Australia's then Prime Minister, Kevin Rudd, officially apologized for the treatment Aboriginal families had received.

☞ Conduct further research into Australia's Stolen Generations. Now imagine it is 2007 (before the official apology in 2008) and you are a descendant of one of the stolen children. Write a letter to the Australian authorities, explaining why you think your people should receive an apology for how they were treated.

The Hon Kevin Rudd MP
Prime Minister
Parliament House
CANBERRA ACT

Dear Mr Rudd,

The birth of a nation

☞ Below is a series of cartoons that tell the story of the birth of a nation – Australia! Cut out the cartoons and stick them on a separate piece of A4 paper in the correct order. Next to each cartoon write down the date, choosing from the list below, and write a description of what event each cartoon is depicting.

Dates
- 1770 • 1788 • 1790 • 1803 • 1840 • 1851
- 1851 • 1855 • 1859 • 1890 • 1891 • 1901

Extension Activity: Can you add any further dates after 1901 that are important in Australia's history?

72   Depth Study: A land down under   © Oxford University Press (copiable page)

Australia word square

☞ Read the clues below. See if you can work out the answers by using the word square grid – the top letter is the first letter of the answer, the left-hand letter is a letter that appears somewhere in the word and the right-hand letter is the last letter of the answer. Use the Student's Book to help you.

1. A term meaning 'land belonging to no one': _____
2. The man responsible for discovering Australia: _____
3. The British believed that the natives didn't farm land like them, which made them _____
4. The people living in Australia before the British arrived: _____
5. The naval commander sent to set up a settlement on Australian soil: _____
6. The men sent from Britain's overcrowded jails to Australia: _____
7. The name given to the 11 ships that travelled to Australia: _____
8. These first ships were known as the _____ of Australia.
9. All convicts were assigned one of these, to whom they reported: _____
10. The name given to 26 January by some Australians: _____

What about New Zealand?

☞ Carefully study the source below which shows the signing of the Treaty of Waitangi. Now imagine you have to report on what went on in this room to the waiting public outside. Even today cameras are not allowed inside UK courts; therefore reporters have to do a good job to explain to television viewers or newspaper readers what happened. You need to provide as much detail as possible to paint a picture for the people who couldn't be there to witness it: imagine you were there in that very room!

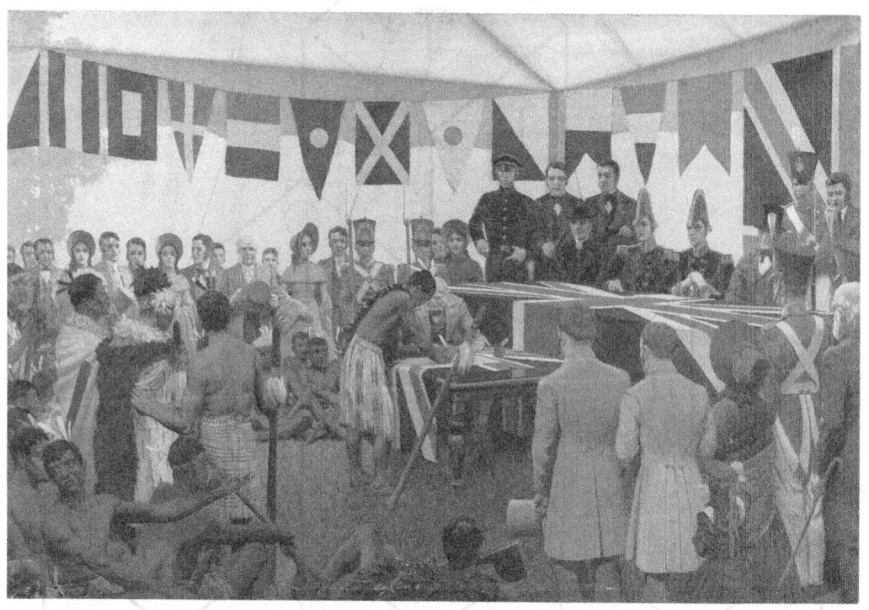

The Australian story

Complete the following fact file. There are also fact files on America and India so you can consider the similarities and differences between these parts of the British Empire from the time early settlers arrived to the events that formed history.

FACT FILE: The Australian Story

When was Australia discovered? _____

How was it discovered? _____

By whom? _____

What happened as the British arrived?

What was it like for the early settlers?

What did Australia have to offer the British?

What interesting facts have you learnt?

© Oxford University Press (copiable page) — Depth study: A land down under 75

The Empire strikes back

☞ This map shows the areas around the world where the British met resistance to the British Empire. Cut out the map and stick it onto an A3 piece of paper. Using the Student's Book and the Internet to help you, think about each of the headings given below and explain how they caused problems for the British by writing around the map and drawing an image to represent each piece of information. Remember to think about: Where? What control did they have? What skills did they have? How were they defeated? Defeat or peace?

The Maroons   The Flagpole War   Easter Rising

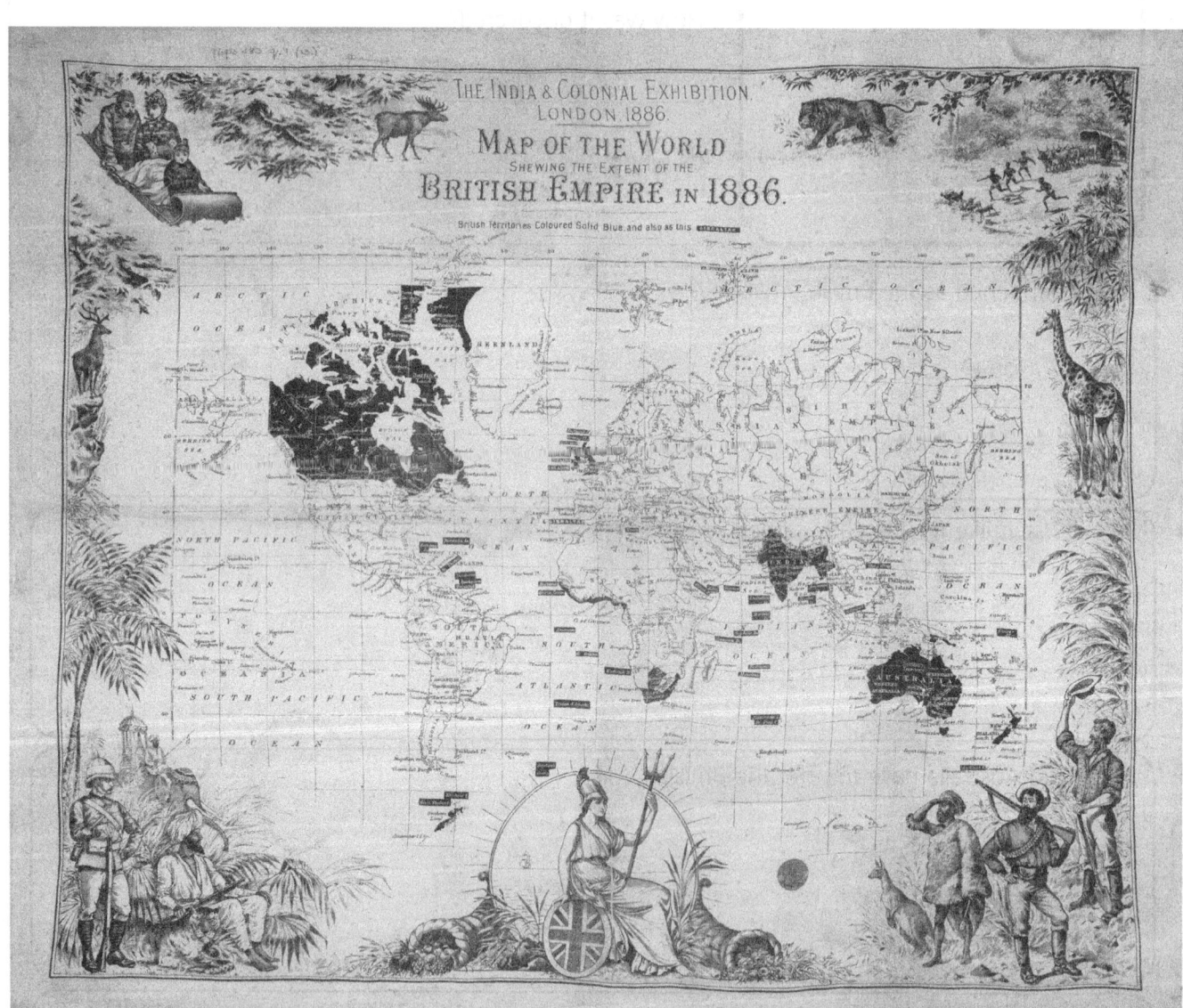

The Boxer Rebellion   The Afghan disaster

The Big Question: Did the Empire strike back?

Who were they?

These two men were awarded the top bravery medals by the British government – but what are their stories?

Khudada Khan was awarded the Victoria Cross in 1914.

Ulric Cross was awarded a Distinguished Flying Cross and a Distinguished Service Order.

☞ **Conduct some research about one of these two men and then write a magazine article about them in a series of question and answers.**

Remember to include the following:
- where they are from
- information about their past and background
- their families
- what they were awarded their medals for
- how they feel about it.

© Oxford University Press (copiable page)

The Big Question: Did the Empire help win two World Wars?

The Empire needs you!

☞ Below are two recruitment posters that were produced to encourage people in the British Empire's colonies to fight for Britain. Study them carefully and answer the following questions.

1. What does this poster show and why? _____
_____
_____

2. How does it encourage people to enlist? _____
_____
_____

3. What does it promise? _____
_____
_____

4. How effective do you think it is? _____
_____
_____

1. How is this poster different? _____
_____
_____

2. What is it trying to do? _____
_____
_____

3. What does it show? _____
_____
_____

4. How effective is it? _____
_____
_____

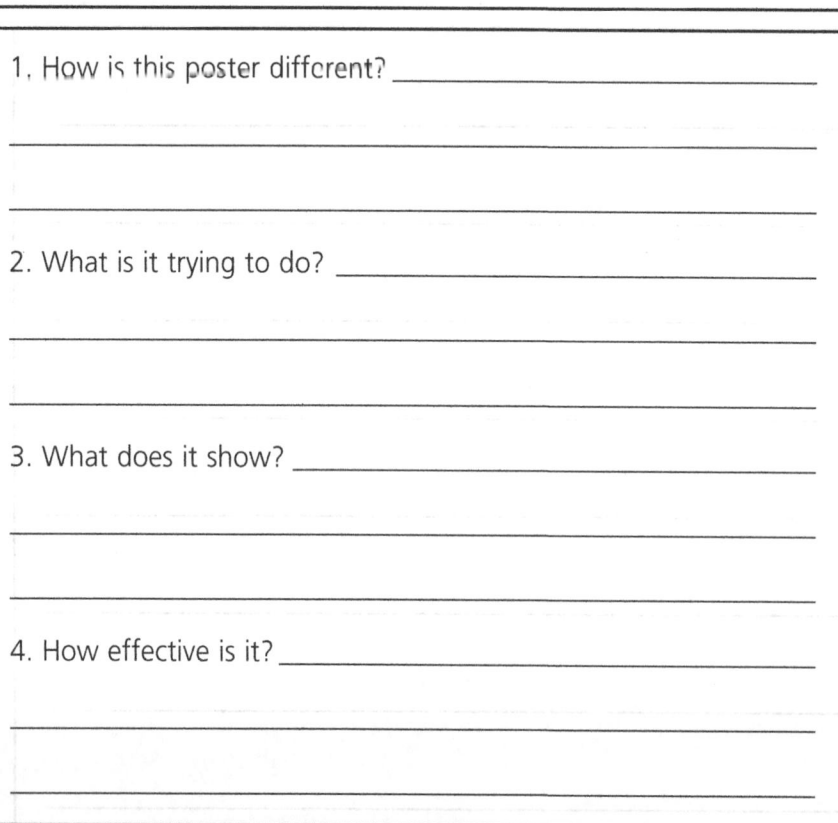

Extension Activity: Now try to produce your own recruitment poster to encourage as many people as possible to enlist in the army.

The Big Question: Did the Empire help win two World Wars?

Africa wordsearch

☞ The following words about Africa can be found in the wordsearch below. Look carefully to see if you can find them all. When you have completed the wordsearch write a brief description of each word.

Word Bank

- Scramble • Zanzibar • Livingstone • Rhodes • Nigeria • Egypt • Maxim • Kenya
- Zulu • Cetshwayo • Shaka • Isandlwana • Rorke's Drift • Boer • Scorched earth
- Ghana • Independence • Apartheid • Commonwealth • Raw materials

E	G	H	A	N	A	M	Q	A	I	R	E	G	I	N
T	G	F	R	G	H	A	N	N	A	A	G	L	N	S
F	A	Y	N	E	K	X	R	A	F	W	U	A	D	C
I	E	B	P	R	A	I	G	W	Y	M	H	P	E	O
R	P	C	S	T	X	M	E	L	P	A	T	A	P	R
D	D	R	H	O	D	E	S	D	S	T	L	R	E	C
S	C	R	A	M	B	L	E	N	Y	E	A	T	N	H
E	M	T	L	I	V	Z	P	A	F	R	E	H	D	E
K	J	C	B	O	B	M	H	S	O	I	W	E	E	D
R	O	K	A	I	L	O	H	I	A	A	N	I	N	E
O	Y	A	W	H	S	T	E	C	K	L	O	D	C	A
R	Z	A	N	Z	I	B	A	R	A	S	M	T	E	R
U	C	U	K	S	N	J	K	A	H	W	M	G	I	T
T	D	V	L	I	V	I	N	G	S	T	O	N	E	H
A	N	E	X	U	W	Z	M	V	N	J	C	W	U	X

© Oxford University Press (copiable page)   Depth Study: Africa   79

Britain's African Empire

☞ Carefully read the clues and write the answers in the grid. You will find the name of a famous British explorer down the middle (Clue 12). Write a paragraph about him including how he helped start the scramble for Africa.

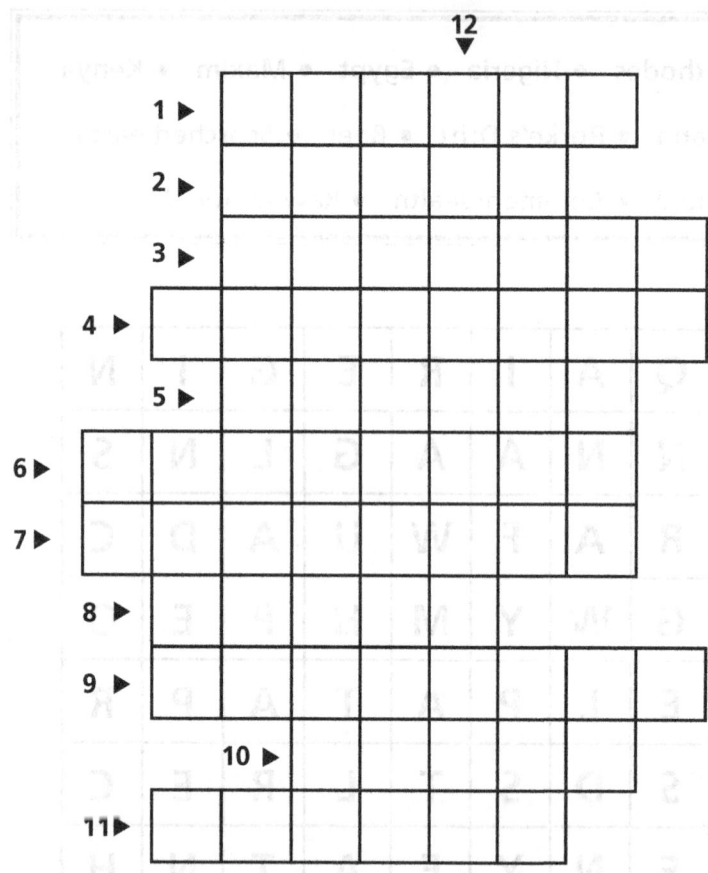

Clues

1. Location of an 1884 conference to discuss the scramble.
2. First name of the first British ruler of Rhodesia.
3. Profitable trade for Britain between 1562 and 1807.
4. Location of the shortest war in history.
5. Britain's main rival in the scramble.
6. New weapon invented in the 1880s.
7. British colonies in Africa: Northern and Southern 8. British colony in North Africa.
9. Very valuable African raw material.
10. Suez _____.
11. 'Bouncy' African raw material.

Clue 12 _____

Zulu (1)

☞ Over the next two pages is a series of cartoons telling the remarkable story of the Zulu's battle with the British on Wednesday 22 January 1879, but they are in the wrong order. Cut them out and stick them onto a piece of A3 paper in the correct order and create a caption for each image to tell the story in your own words.

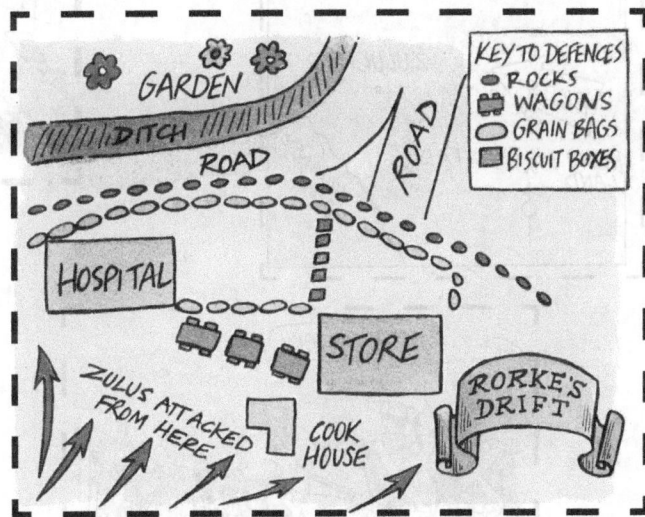

© Oxford University Press (copiable page)   Depth Study: Africa

Zulu (2)

An historical snapshot

☞ Pictured below is a famous painting that provides a snapshot of a very important day in the history of the British Empire. Imagine you are the curator of a museum which has been given this painting as a gift. Prepare a visitor information pack about it so that visitors to the museum can gain an insight into what is happening in the painting.

The place shown in the painting	What is happening in the painting

What events led up to this scene occurring	A description of any key figures

The story of Pip the dog

© Oxford University Press (copiable page)   Depth Study: Africa   83

Unfit for duty

The Boer War was Britain's biggest Empire war. Nearly 500,000 Brits fought in it and 8000 died; another 13,000 died due to illness. Many of the men that fought for the British were classed as 'unfit for duty'. So what was done to make improvements to secure the health of the British population?

☞ Using the library, the Internet and your class notes research the improvements that were made in order to ensure the British government had a fit population in case they were needed to fight a war again.

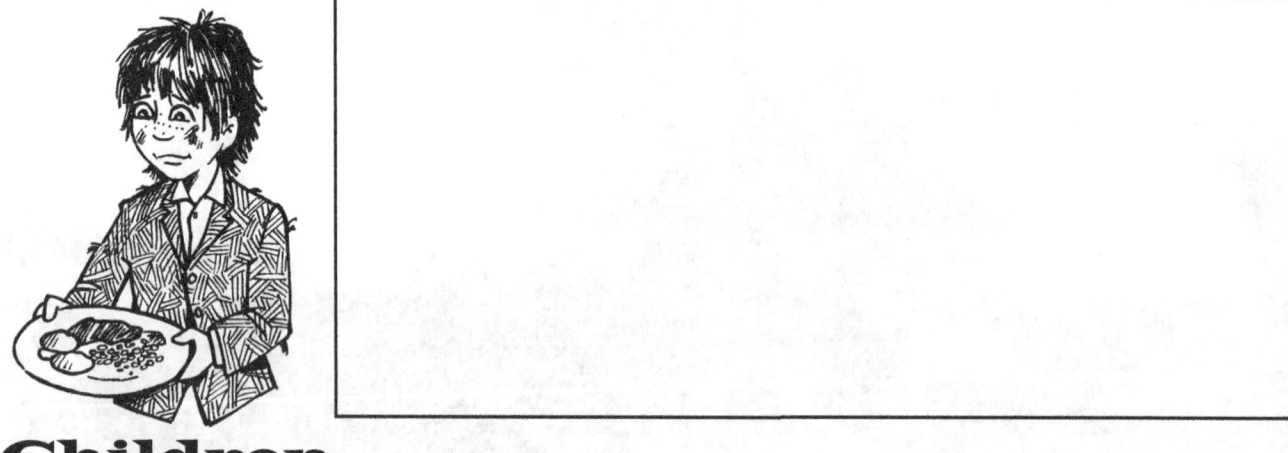

Children

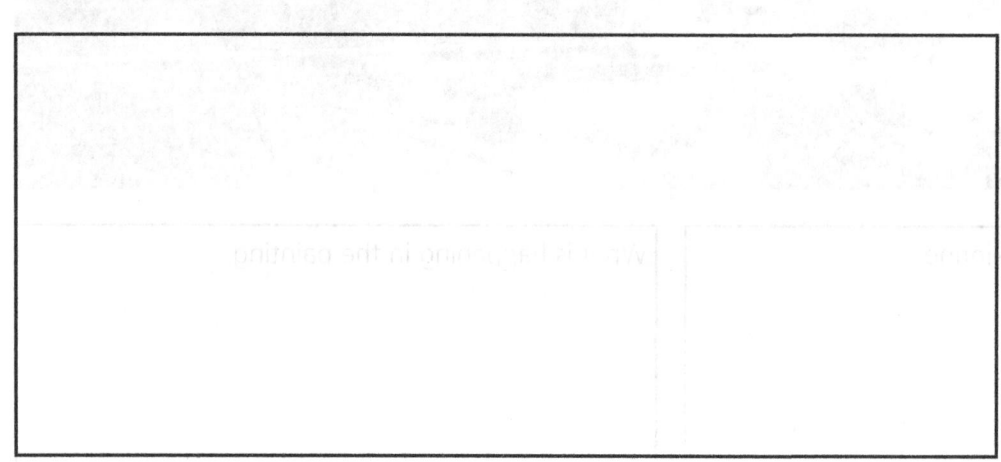

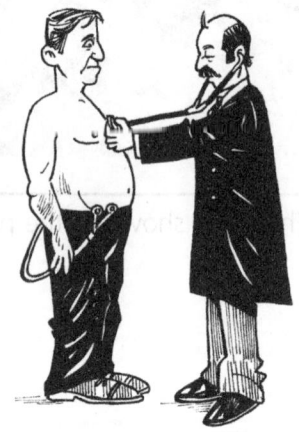

Health

Employment

The Big Question: What is the legacy of the British Empire?

Legacy of the Empire

☞ Despite the fact that the British Empire doesn't exist any more, its legacy still survives in different parts of the world today. But what did the British leave behind? Use the boxes provided to explain the British legacy.

Commonwealth

Democracy

Sport

Law

Language

Extension Activity: See if you can find out what other benefits remain from British rule. Think about the things the British built when they ruled.

Positive or negative?

☞ The following statements show differing opinions about the British Empire. Cut out each one and divide them into positive opinions and negative opinions. Stick them into your workbook and explain in your own words a little more about what each person means based on what you have learnt about the British Empire.

The Big Question: Was the British Empire a good or a bad thing?

British overseas territories

☞ There are still 14 British colonies in existence today, but where are they and why do they remain British? Complete the map below by labelling the 14 colonies and then find out a few facts about at least eight of them. See if you can find out *why* they remain part of the British overseas territory.

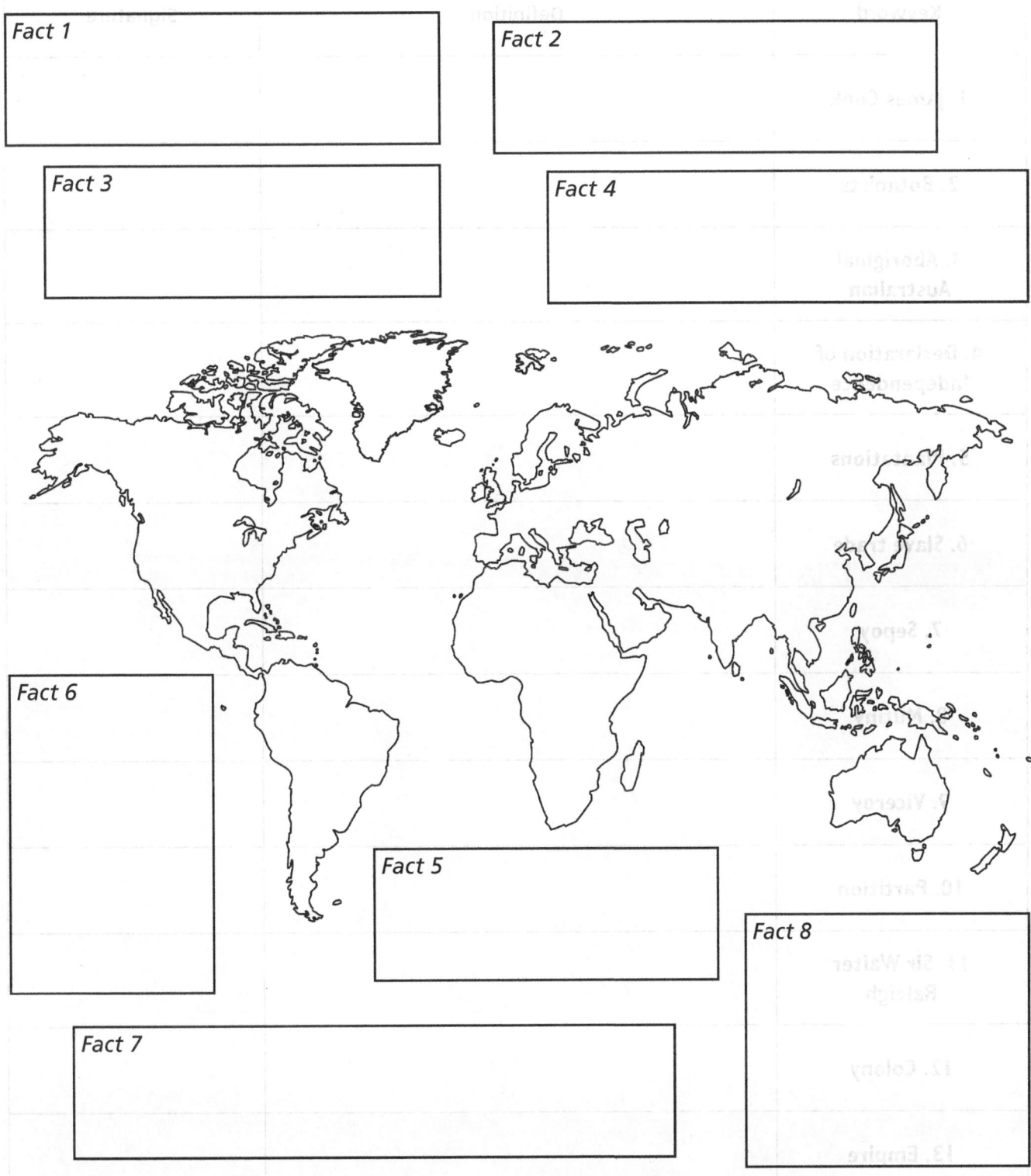

Fact 1	Fact 2
Fact 3	Fact 4
Fact 6	Fact 5
	Fact 8
Fact 7	

Extension Activity: Think carefully about the people who still live in these colonies today. Are they influenced by the British? Do they speak the same language? Think about what reasons the British had for invading the area in the first place.

© Oxford University Press (copiable page)

The Big Question: Was the British Empire a good or a bad thing?

Get out of your seats!

☞ Complete the table below by asking people what each word or phrase means – you can only use one person per answer! Write their answer in the table and get them to sign their name: see if they know as much as you!

Keyword	Definition	Signature
1. James Cook		
2. Botanists		
3. Aboriginal Australian		
4. Declaration of Independence		
5. Plantations		
6. Slave trade		
7. Sepoy		
8. Mutiny		
9. Viceroy		
10. Partition		
11. Sir Walter Raleigh		
12. Colony		
13. Empire		
14. Christopher Columbus		

The Big Question: Was the British Empire a good or a bad thing?